THE FEMININE UNIVERSE
A Manifesto of Feminine Essentialism

THIS IS NO ORDINARY BOOK. It will either leave you wholly unmoved, or it will transform your life forever.

In a fragmented world full of conflicting ideas and alternatives, this book puts forward the other point of view. The one that is other than all of them. The only real alternative there is.

Necessarily the conceptual leap needed to transfer one's thoughts from the late patriarchal universe to the primordial feminine cosmos is considerable, but Miss Trent has an extraordinary gift for expressing complex and unfamiliar ideas in a way that is crystalline in its lucidity and divine in its simplicity.

If you have ever felt something was deeply wrong with the world, but were not sure what, this book will make it transparently clear.

If you have ever felt that you knew *you* could make your own life better, and perhaps the world about you, this book shows how right you were, and how you can go about it.

COVER PICTURE: The Cosmic Maid *by Giacomella Daqui depicts the cosmos embodied as a maiden encompassing the celestial spheres. We see the Sphere of Earth enclosed by the Sphere of the Moon and beyond the other Spheres and the Fixed Stars. The cloak of the Cosmic Maid falls within the Sphere of Earth and is figured with roses and clouds— roses which are symbolic of Fire and grow in the Earth; clouds which are compounded of Air and Water, thus figuring the four elements and all the earthly fecundity to which they give rise. She is crowned with the Sun, in symbol of the Solar nature of Maid.*

This picture illustrates the Aristasian ideal of Neo-Traditional art comprising Archetypal motifs *depicted in the legitimate modern stylized manner of Art Neo.*

*Sri Yantra: an image of the Universe, and of
the Supreme Mother God in Her Trinitarian
form as Tripura Sundari, the Beauty of the
Three Worlds*

THE FEMININE
UNIVERSE

A Complete Outline of the Primordial

Feminine Essentialist Philosophy

By Miss Alice Lucy Trent

THE GOLDEN ORDER PRESS
an imprint of
The Sun Daughter Press

Other books by
THE SUN DAUGHTER PRESS
(The Feminine Publishing Company)

The Gospel of Our Mother God
Sappho: 100 Lyrics ed. Sushuri Madonna-chei
Enter Amelia Bingham by Geneviève Falconer
The Flight of the Silver Vixen by Annalinde Matichei

––––––––––––

The Feminine Universe
Published by
THE GOLDEN ORDER PRESS
an imprint of
THE SUN DAUGHTER PRESS

First published 1997
This first American edition published 2010

CONTENTS

There is only one mythology, one iconology, and one truth; that of an uncreated wisdom that has been handed down from time immemorial.

ANANDA COOMARASWAMY

The term philosophia perennis, *which has been current since the time of the Renaissance... signifies the totality of the primordial and universal truths—and therefore of metaphysical axioms—whose formulation does not belong to any particular system.*

FRITHJOF SCHUON

In truth pure metaphysics is neither Eastern nor Western, but universal... [the] forms may be Eastern or Western, but under the appearance of diversity there is always a basis of unity, at least wherever true metaphysics exists, for the simple reason that truth is one.

RENÉ GUÉNON

The traditional approach to reality is everywhere and always the same, despite the great differences in the historical development of traditional civilizations.

LORD NORTHBOURNE

INTRODUCTION

THIS BOOK is the first systematic exposition of the Perennial Wisdom. It is an attempt to express in the clearest possible terms and in the smallest possible space the Primordial Philosophy accepted and understood in all times and in all places before the aberrations of the modern world. It gives this philosophy in its feminine form—that being the earliest known on this earth.

Ananda Coomaraswamy described traditional societies as "unanimous societies": that is, societies not fragmented by conflicting factions and opinions, but united by a single, essential Truth.

And this unanimity exists—though often unrecognized[1]—not only *within* all traditional societies, from the American medicine lodge to the Chinese temple, from the Siberian shaman to the Indian guru, from the Platonic West to the Confucian East, but *between* all traditional societies. Each one is founded upon the same essential, unchanging truths, even though they may express these truths in superficially different ways. Each one is a unique expression of the *Sophia Perennis*, the primordial, changeless, and eternal wisdom that is the common heritage of all humanity.

While many books have been written about this Primordial Tradition, this is the first one to expound it systematically in its salient features. That alone would make it a book of the greatest

---

1. In fact the universality of tradition *is* largely recognized outside the exclusivism of the three Semitic monotheisms, Judaism, Christianity, and Islam—the most recent of the world's religions. Marco Pallis, traveling in the East, was frequently asked by spiritual people: "And to what noble Tradition do you belong?" The more traditional mind has no difficulty in grasping that Truth may speak many 'languages' without ceasing to be the same Truth. Even Islam is not only able to recognize other 'religions of the Book'—i.e., Semitic monotheisms—but in India to recognize that Hinduism too is such a religion, the *Bhagavad Gita* being no less The Book than the Hebrew scriptures. And even St. Augustine, the most authoritative of the early Christian Fathers, writes: "The very thing that is now called the Christian religion was not wanting among the ancients from the beginning of the human race". Clearly he does not mean that Christianity existed in its present outward form before Christ, but that behind the outward form, the Truth is always and everywhere the same [*vide* Stephen Cross, "St. Augustine and the Perennial Philosophy" in *Avaloka: a Journal of Traditional Religion and Culture*, Vol. VI, nos. 1 & 2].

significance, but, within a very short space, this book does much
more than that. It also discusses the essentially feminine nature of
the earliest traditions and shows the importance of this in the
development of the historical cycle and its special relevance to
the developments of the last few decades.

Writers such as René Guénon and Ananda Coomaraswamy
have expounded the *Sophia Perennis* in many volumes. They have
done so from a purely metaphysical and Traditional perspective
(which is necessarily the highest and truest). While this book certainly expounds metaphysical Truth, which is indeed its very core,
it also examines the consequences and ramifications of traditional
thought from a lower, more 'human' perspective.

From the 'pure' perspective of Guénon or Coomaraswamy it is
necessary to reject out of hand the Western world that has come
into being since the European Renaissance, or certainly since the
mid-seventeenth century. Guénon writes:

> . . . *what characterizes the final phase of a cycle is the exploitation*
> *of everything that has been neglected or rejected during the course*
> *of the preceding phases; and indeed this is precisely what is to be*
> *observed in modern civilization, which only lives, so to speak, by*
> *things which previous civilizations found no use for.*
>
> *Crisis of the Modern World*

This poses certain questions. Are we, for example, to include
the works of Beethoven, Mozart, Keats, and Wordsworth, and even
Michelangelo, among the "rejected elements", the "things which
previous civilizations found no use for", of which Guénon speaks?
Indeed, we must. But to say that they are "rejected elements" is not
necessarily to say that they are worthless and contemptible. It may
be to say that they are the Final Fruits of the Historical Cycle,
manifesting possibilities of a lower order than was possible in previous phases, but which nonetheless are good and beautiful in their
own right and without which the Cycle would be incomplete.

This book takes a fresh look at post-Enlightenment culture with this
in mind, analyzing both its faults and its virtues, and shows how even
up to the earlier twentieth century the Traditional spirit remained
vital in the aesthetic and cultural life of the Western world. What is
necessary is to distinguish between those 'modern' developments that are

legitimate Final Fruits and those that are truly malignant aberrations.

In the light of this, the book examines phenomena that Guénon and Coomaraswamy did not live to see and comment on: the cultural collapse of the 1960s with its complete inversion of normal values, and most terrible of all, the destruction of femininity and the creation of an unbalanced world in which the Masculine Principle has come to dominate the culture absolutely, extirpating femininity even from the heart of woman herself. This book explains the traditional value of femininity and its essential superiority. It exposes the modern attack on femininity and the absurd doctrine that this cosmic Reality is the result of 'social conditioning'. It shows how what is being lost by the totalitarian imposition of an all-masculine culture is something of immeasurable importance to our spiritual health and our very survival.

Note that the scientific evidence presented in Chapter Four does not consist of 'selected facts'. Anyone who cares to speak to those involved in neuroscience research will quickly discover that there is *no* 'opposition' within the field. Despite the almost universal acceptance of the 'social conditioning' theory of femininity by the lay public, there are *no* neuroscientists who can any longer sustain this. Modern brain-scan technology has made it visibly and unarguably clear that the female brain is radically different from the male brain and that the psychological characteristics that necessarily flow from this are precisely those of 'conventional' femininity. No informed person can any longer dispute this, any more than she can dispute the roundness of the earth. The continued belief in the 'social conditioning' theory of femininity is simply an example of the 'ideological ignorance' of an over-politicized society.

What we must understand is that from the Traditional point of view, these feminine characteristics are in fact the *highest* of human characteristics and that our rejection of them not only does violence to the inborn nature of women, but impoverishes society and robs it of its vital center.

We ask readers to note that the 'universal she' is used throughout this book in place of the traditional patriarchal 'he'. We do this for precisely the same reason that 'he' is used by patriarchal writers (or rather the reverse of that reason)—because we regard the female as the primary or fundamental sex; and in this, as we shall see, we are borne out by history, biology, and metaphysics.

9

The religion of the prehistoric and early historical world was a mono-theism in which the female form of divinity was supreme.

SIR ARTHUR EVANS

It is remarkable that the many varied and highly expert author-archaeologists in the excellent series Ancient People and Places *express their wonder at the evidence they have found that women were once pre-eminent in each of their areas of research, from the Near East to Ireland. Each writes as if this ancient dominance of women were unique and peculiar to his archaeological province. Yet taken all together these archaeological finds prove that feminine pre-eminence was a universal, and not a localized, phenomenon.*

ELIZABETH GOULD DAVIS

[Our present civilization stems from] *a common cultural inheritance throughout an area extending from Mesopotamia to Egypt and the Ganges to the Mediterranean,* [founded upon] *the worship of the Great Mother.*

ANANDA COOMARASWAMY

THE FEMININE HERITAGE

"When above the heavens had not been formed, when the earth below had no name, Tiamat brought forth them both. Tiamat, Mother of the gods, Creator of all."

SO BEGINS the earliest known account of the creation of the world.[1]

Moving from the Near East to Europe, the earliest known creation story is the pre-Hellenic Pelasgian Creation Myth, which depicts the creation of the universe by Eurynome, the Goddess of All Things. Commenting on this in his classic study of the Greek myths, Robert Graves says: "In this archaic religious system there were as yet neither gods nor priests, but only a universal goddess and her priestesses, woman being the dominant sex."[2]

In all myth throughout the world, the original Creator is feminine. It is only with the coming of a masculine-dominated (patriarchal) social system that She is replaced by a male god. Sometimes (as in the case of Tiamat above) She is said to have been conquered or killed by the new god. Sometimes the patriarchy boldly changed the sex of the Deity without changing the name—as with Ea in Syria, Shiva in India or Atea in Polynesia. Sometimes the goddess was slowly edged out and the god edged in. W. R. Smith points out that the goddesses of the ancient Semites "changed their sex and became gods" in historical times[3] while Atea, the supreme God of Polynesia, was a Goddess as little as 500 years ago.[4]

Often the new cult of the male god could only be made to replace the original religion of the Goddess by a very severe patriarchal regime. This was the case with the Hebrew Jehovah.[5] Even then, the people frequently reverted to the worship of "the Queen of Heaven", much to the chagrin of the patriarchal prophets.[6]

---

1. *The Enuma Elish* (earliest text) Tr. Muss-Arnolt.
2. Robert Graves, *The Greek Myths,* Penguin, Vol. I, p.2.
3. In Theodor Reik, *Pagan Rites in Judaism,* Farrar, p.7.
4. Peter N. Buck, *Vikings of the Pacific,* University of Chicago Press, p.735.
5. Reik, op. cit., p.101.
6. e.g., Jeremiah. Ch. 44, vv. 16-19.

Turning from the 'historical' to the 'prehistoric' period—that is to say, to that vast majority of human history for which written records no longer exist or have been rewritten by patriarchal redactors—the material evidence makes it clear that the religion of the feminine Deity was predominant for thousands of years.

James Mellaart, probably the world's foremost authority on Near Eastern archaeology, writes in his famous survey of ancient Near Eastern civilization: "Between 9000 and 7000 B.C. art makes its appearance in the Near East in the form of statuettes of the supreme deity, the Great Goddess."[7] Mellaart states that historically "the cult of the Great Goddess" is "the basis of our civilization".[8]

In a similar survey of ancient European civilization between 7000 and 3500 B.C., Professor Marija Gimbutas explains how recent archaeology has given us a clear picture of this period, unearthing some 30,000 sculptures of clay, marble, bone, copper, and gold from some 3,000 sites. Clearly a vast area and a great period of time are involved (much longer than the whole known 'historical' period), yet certain general statements can be made covering the entire civilization. Prof. Gimbutas shows that the Creator of the world was regarded as a Goddess (like Tiamat, often symbolized as a bird), that the Great Goddess was "the central figure in the pantheon of gods" and that "the pantheon reflects a society dominated by the mother".[9]

We may go back further, say to the Gravettian-Aurignacian cultures, sites of which have been found in Spain, France, Germany, Austria, Czechoslovakia, and Russia, and recently as far afield as Anatolia in the Near East. Some of these sites date back well over 25,000 years, and in these virtually all statues, divine or human, are female.

In the period after 9000 B.C., the pattern tended to follow that stated by Mellaart in connexion with ancient Hacilar (c. 5800 B.C.): "The statuettes portray the Goddess and the male appears only in a subsidiary rôle." But in the older Gravettian-Aurignacian cultures,

---

7. James Mellaart, *Earliest Civilizations of the Near East*, McGraw Hill, p.18.
8. Ibid p.77.
9. Marija Gimbutas, *The Gods and Goddesses of Old Europe, 7000-3500 B.C.*, Thames & Hudson, pp. 236-237.

the male scarcely appears at all. What we have is a vast preponderance of stylized female images, known to archaeologists as "Venus figures".

We might go back further still, for example to the Venus of the Wildenmannisloch Cave, which is at least seventy thousand years old, but as we recede into such distant eras, dating and interpretation obviously become more difficult and conservative scholarship becomes cautious. Let us, therefore, remain with the wealth of well-attested and generally accepted fact.

What were they like, these prehistoric civilizations? Archaeologists refer to them as Palaeolithic (old stone age), Neolithic (new stone age), and so on—terms that to the average person imply brutish 'cave men' dressed in skins and barely able to speak. Serious archaeologists have not believed in this popular myth for well over half a century now, and the discoveries of the last twenty years in Europe and the Near East have shown that it is so far from the truth as to be ridiculous.

Let us take Hacilar, mentioned above in connexion with the predominance of the female image. This 'stone-age' community lived in two-story houses, often thirty feet in length, arranged about a central courtyard, with ovens, kitchens, hearths upstairs and down, verandas overlooking the courtyard, and numerous other "civilized" features.[10]

This example is entirely typical. We find similar conditions all over Neolithic Europe and the Near East and as far afield as Dravidian India. Furthermore, these societies were not separate developments, but as the great Indologist Ananda Coomaraswamy points out, the fruits of "a common cultural inheritance throughout an area extending from Mesopotamia to Egypt and the Ganges to the Mediterranean" based upon "the worship of the Great Mother".[11]

It was a matriarchal civilization in which the priesthood, the heads of families and of State were all female. The concept of feminine supremacy is so alien to modern minds that many male scholars have described it in terms that imply abject subjection

10. Mellaart, *The Neolithic of the Near East,* Thames & Hudson, pp.111-113.
11. Coomaraswamy, *A University Course in Indian Art,* Raja Singam, p.34.

on the part of men. Speaking of Catal Huyuk, the oldest town at present known to archaeology, Mellaart, who was the excavator, speaks of "man's subservience to woman".[12] Charles Seltman says of the pre-Mycenaean Greeks: "religion and custom were dominated by the female principle, and men were but the servers of women".[13] Graves says that men, as the "weaker sex" "could be trusted to hunt, fish, gather certain foods, mind flocks and herds... so long as they did not transgress matriarchal law".[14] J. J. Bachofen says that in prehistoric times "woman towers above man", and speaks of "the contrast between the dominant woman and the servile man".[15]

This assumption of man's abject condition in the ancient world is but the result of an ingrained patriarchal prejudice which baulks at the overturning of his 'natural' superiority. To an unprejudiced eye, what emerges is a picture of a peaceful civilization of small towns, villages, and a few small cities, based on a common religion and philosophy, and where, under clear feminine leadership, "all the resources of human nature, feminine and masculine, were utilized to the full as a creative force."[16]

It is also likely, judging from the complete absence, rather than subordinacy, of the male image, that, at least in many places, the center of civilization was a predominantly feminine affair in which men played little part, and in which relations between women, at least among the upper echelons of society, were considered more important than their relations with men. This would be parallel with the pattern in patriarchal societies such as ancient Athens, pre-twentieth century academic communities, religious hierarchies, and so forth.

Note for the new American Edition: One frequently hears comments to the effect that "the once-popular theory of ancient matriarchy has now been discredited by scholars". The truth behind this statement is simply this. Scholars have declared, rightly, that there is no evidence

---

12. Mellaart, *Catal Huyuk*, McGraw Hill, p.184.
13. Seltman, *The Twelve Olympians*, Apollo, p.27.
14. Graves, op. cit., I, p.15.
15. Bachofen, *Myth, Religion and Mother Right*, Princeton University Press, p.112.
16. Marija Gimbutas, op. cit., p.238.

that earlier civilizations were actually ruled by women. This is perfectly true, for there are no written records extant for these periods (which constitute a length of history many times greater than the whole era of patriarchy) and it is impossible to be certain what their social institutions were. What is quite clear is that in their iconography they were almost exclusively feminine-oriented.

And let us be very clear that archaeological finds in the twenty-first century have continued to establish that the iconography of earlier pre-historic societies, from the Americas to Japan, *was* almost exclusively feminine. Some scholars have come up with remarkable attempts to discount this (one reputable scholar suggested that perhaps certain early Japanese figurines were not feminine as "some men have breasts"!) but apart from such entertaining asides, which only serve to demonstrate the depth of patriarchal prejudice, the body of evidence continues to confirm and consolidate the findings of this chapter.

Nevertheless, the modern scholar takes it as axiomatic that female rule is inherently unlikely (this from people who otherwise argue that the differences between men and women are purely 'socially conditioned', and therefore ought logically to believe that a different set of 'conditioning' would produce a different social order) and that the burden of proof rests with those who claim that female rule ever existed. "If it cannot be proved, we may assume it did not exist, as it is, after all, most improbable" is the unspoken 'scholarly' assumption behind this, which is quickly expanded to "the theory of matriarchy has been discredited by scholars" in less rigorous contexts.

Knowing what we do of the way traditional peoples always or-ganize their social activities and institutions in imitation of (in the words of the great anthropologist Mircea Eliade) "Those things first done by the gods", we should say that the very distinction between iconography, religion, and social organization is a purely modern one that only a Rajasic-era mind could conceive of. Feminine-dominated iconography, for any traditional people, must imply a feminine-dominated society. In our view the burden of proof rests heavily upon the anti-matriarchy school. The existence of matriarchy is by far the most probable and reasonable hypothesis until and unless someone comes up with a shred of evidence against it.

Chapter One

THE IMAGE OF THE COSMOS

The total nature of the world is… to all eternity chaos, not in the sense that necessity is lacking, but in that order, structure, form, beauty, wisdom, and whatever other human aesthetic notions we may have are lacking… Let us beware of attributing to it heartlessness and unreason or their opposites: it is neither perfect nor beautiful nor noble, and has no desire to become any of these… neither does it know any laws. Let us beware of saying there are laws in nature. There are only necessities. There is no one to command, no one to obey, no one to transgress… Let us beware of saying that death is the opposite of life. The living being is only a species of the dead, and a very rare species.

NIETZSCHE

THE QUOTATION above states the modern view of the universe, shared by almost everyone alive today.

Certainly it is expressed more frankly—more brutally—than most people would care to put it. But this cold, void, chaotic vision of the ultimate nature of things is the underlying image of the modern world-picture. It is the foundation-stone upon which the twentieth century constructed its view of the universe; and it explains many things about the way people in current Western societies feel and behave.

For the way we see the universe is not separate from the way we see ourselves. If our cosmos is chaotic and meaningless, how can we be harmonious and our lives have true purpose? If our cosmos is cold and empty, how can we be otherwise?

Every traditional people has seen humanity and the cosmos as being radically interlinked, and maid herself a *microcosm* or 'little cosmos'—and conversely the cosmos itself as ultimately akin to ourselves. Our very word 'world' (*wer ald*) means originally 'the great man', and, of course, in the earliest times, the Cosmic Maid was conceived as feminine. We and the cosmos are related in traditional thought; are of the same Essence and the same substance. We are both intelligible and we both *mean* the same things.

Conversely, according to the modern view, we are but an accident in the vastness of the cosmos; we might not have been, or we might have been quite otherwise. Within the infinite galaxies we are but an insignificant speck, and within the endless vistas of cosmic time, our whole history, past, present, and future, is but a moment; and a moment of no special significance. Above all, we have nothing in common with the cosmos; it is alien to us, knows nothing of our values or aspirations—knows nothing at all, indeed, for it is but insensate matter, and as accidental and meaningless as ourselves.

When maid loses her significance in the cosmos, and the cosmos loses its significance around her, many other things are also lost. Until very recently maid walked in the knowledge that she was a little universe, and every move she made, each word she spoke, the clothes she wore and the things with which she surrounded herself all reflected this.

Picture the maid of the present moment, in loose and baggy clothes, striving always for the odd and the grotesque, or else for the casual and the careless. Does she not represent her picture of the universe? Aimless, accidental, chaotic, ultimately meaningless? Perhaps her shirt spells out some vulgar joke or advertises a commercial product. Why not? For what dignity can she aspire to: an accidental fleck floating for a brief moment in a world of random dust?

Her clothes are the clothes of self-mockery and demoralization. Her life, cut off from all sources of meaning and harmony, becomes an aimless wandering, spiced only by the endless artificial wants stimulated by the commercial system; and by those desires we share with dogs and cats, raised to the status of gods and stimulated by every means available to mass-communication.

And as our universe disintegrates from a unified, meaningful whole into a congeries of unrelated objects separated by unfathomable distances of cold black space, so our social fabric is unwoven, the ties of loyalty and love, of tradition and trust unloose, leaving each individual increasingly an isolated unit fending for herself in a cold and alien world.

Many other consequences spring from this new vision of the world as meaningless and empty—not least a loss of our old sense of responsibility toward the world. For if we are nothing to the world and the world is nothing to us; if maid is not a little world, nor the world a great maid, why should we treat her with respect? Why should we not plunder and destroy her? Once the bonds of meaning and loyalty and the dance of eternal harmony are gone, even common self-preservation, it seems, will not suffice to stop us sawing off the branch on which we sit.

We may think of ourselves as animals; and of animals as mere machines programmed for survival: but when this animal survival is all, when what have always been our specifically *human* beliefs and motivations have been stripped from us, it transpires that we are not even very good at being animals, and do not greatly care about survival itself.

*

But even if we agree that we are better off with an intelligible cosmos, a cosmos that reflects maid herself—or rather, of which she is a reflection —that does not help us in the least, if we cannot believe it to be true.

Various people have suggested that it would be better for humanity to return to some of its earlier myths and meanings; to end the emptiness and chaos of a random accidental world. Such suggestions in themselves are pointless. We cannot choose to believe something we think to be untrue. We cannot live our lives by pretty lies. It is not in our nature.

Those thinkers who have hoped to redeem the world by myths seen through the eyes of modern anthropology or psychology have missed the point entirely. Modern psychology and anthropology set themselves above myth; seek to explain the super-human in human terms, to reduce the supernatural to an epiphenomenon of nature.

If the traditional mythic visions are true, then they are fundamental. There is no getting 'behind' them. If they are true, then *they* provide the explanations of human culture and the human mind, not *vice versa*. And if they are not true, then they are of no use to us or to anyone.

The modern picture of the universe presents itself as truth. Not attractive or meaningful to us, but simply true. That is the force of Nietzsche's words quoted above. This view claims to have disproved the previous view—to have relegated it to the realms of outdated fantasy. A universe made in the image of maid (or even *vice versa*) was a childish egocentricity of ours. Now we know the truth, whether we like it or not. The cosmos is unrelated to us except inso- far as we are one of its numberless random and fleeting accidents. It has no message for us, no meaning for us. It is unintelligent and unintelligible. It just *is* and no more. We know this as a result of our superior knowledge. Our science has proved all other ages wrong and ourselves right.

Such is the received wisdom of the modern world. But is it true? *Has* the modern 'scientific' world-view disproved the earlier picture of the intelligent, intelligible cosmos? Because if it has not, we may be making a terrible mistake. We may be cutting ourselves loose from our psychic moorings, displacing ourselves from our natural place in the cosmos, wreaking untold psychic damage not only upon ourselves, but—if tradition is right about the intimate connexion between maid and the cosmos—upon the world about us; and all needlessly. Nietzsche saw all too clearly the psychological results of such an inner revolution:

> *Who gave us a sponge to wipe away the entire horizon? What did we do when we unchained this earth from its sun? Whither is it moving now? Whither are we moving now? Away from all suns... Are we not straying as through an infinite nothing? Do we not feel the breath of empty space? Has it not become colder? Is more and more night not coming on all the time?*

Of course, if this new vision is simply *true,* there is nothing we can do about it. The older vision that gave us a place in a friendly and harmonious cosmos has been disproved. We must live with the new truth even if it empty our hearts and souls, even if it destroy the very bonds between maid and maid, kill our respect for ourselves, unstring our love of beauty and of kindness and finally quench the very will to continue living.

If it is simply truc and *if* it has disproved the earlier vision. But has it? The purpose of this book is to set out the traditional view of the cosmos and to show that it has *not* been disproved.

The traditional view? some may ask. Surely there have been many views, many mythologies, many religions before the present. Which of the traditional views are we going to present?

But we reiterate: we are going to present *the* traditional view, for there is really only one. It has been put forward in different spiritual and symbolic languages by different cultures, but in its essence, it is always and everywhere the same.

And we are going to examine the traditional view in its feminine form, which is far older than the masculine version of it known to relatively recent historical cultures. We shall do this for two reasons. First because it *is* the oldest, the primordial, form of the one great human tradition, and secondly because we believe that much of the problem of the world today, including the loss of that tradition, lies in the over-valuation of the masculine as opposed to the feminine.

We have in mind the fact that many women today are looking for answers to the questions that beset our civilization—answers that can only be provided by traditional wisdom—and yet the patriarchal forms which that wisdom has taken in the last few millennia can be alienating to the feminine psyche. Nevertheless, our message is not only for women. In a world starved of the feminine just as it is starved of the higher dimensions of mythic and symbolic truth, we believe the timeless message of the universal Feminine Tradition will come as a healing balm to *all* who are ready to hear it.

But although our focus will be the feminine, nonetheless we shall hold ourselves free to draw on tradition in whatever form we may find it; on the sacred cosmos of the mediaeval West as much as on more ancient forms: for all, as we say, are but dialects of the same language and all are speaking the same truth.

Let us return then to the question we posed a few moments ago. Has the traditional view of the cosmos been disproved and super-seded by the modern view?

Obviously we must begin by asking: what *is* the traditional view?

The form of it most immediately accessible to the modern West is that generally accepted throughout the Classical and Mediaeval periods, up until the Copernican revolution of the seventeenth century.

According to this system, the earth stands at the center of the universe. The earth is a round ball, and beyond it are a series of concentric spheres, transparent and crystalline. Governing each of these spheres is a planet, which is essentially a god or an angel. The first of these spheres, traveling out from the earth, is the Sphere of the Moon, then comes the Sphere of Venus, and so on out to the seventh sphere, the Sphere of Saturn. Beyond this is the Sphere of the Fixed Stars and the very Heaven-world itself.

Now, is this view of the universe true or false? C. S. Lewis, who expounds the traditional image of the cosmos very lucidly in his book *The Discarded Image,* and is clearly highly sympathetic to its beauty and harmony, nevertheless feels himself compelled to admit that it is based on what he terms "exploded astronomy"; on a false, or as some would say 'pre-scientific', understanding of the nature of the physical universe.

This, of course, has been the general consensus of the educated modern world since the seventeenth century, held equally by those who wish contemptuously to sweep aside 'the errors and superstitions of the past', and those like C. S. Lewis who may regret the passing of a more humane and intelligent cosmos, a more poetic and profound vision, but can see no intellectual possibility of reinstating it. For both alike, whether for better or worse, it is, as C. S. Lewis names it, the discarded image.

And they are wrong. The image should never have been discarded. The reasons for which it was rejected were false reasons. The entire process was based on a very simple but very fundamental misunderstanding, and Western maid was alienated from her cosmos, her world drained of depth and significance, as a result of an error of interpretation and a confusion of levels.

The traditional image of the cosmos was *not* based on "exploded astronomy", because it was not based on astronomy at all. It has nothing in common with astronomy in the modern sense of the word—which is to say, with attempts to understand the *physical* universe on a purely *physical* level.

This is in fact perfectly clear from the traditional writings on the cosmos. The sublunary realm—that is, the world below the Sphere of the Moon: our Earth—is the realm of material things; the world of change and decay; in other words, *the physical universe.*

Everything in physical manifestation, that is, everything comprehended by modern astronomy and by modern science as a whole—from the smallest subatomic particle to the furthest galaxy countless light-years away—is part of the first circle of the traditional cosmos.

As soon as we reach the very nearest of the celestial Spheres, the Sphere of the Moon, we are already beyond the material world and beyond everything recognized by physical science.

To say that traditional cosmology has been "exploded" by modern astronomy is on the same level of non sequitur as the statement once encountered in popular atheist pamphlets: "As a doctor I can assure you that there is no life after death." A doctor may reasonably claim a greater knowledge of the workings of the human body than a layman. On questions that transcend the physical realm he has no greater claim than anyone else; and to assert his knowledge in one area as a guarantee of his speculations in another is nothing more than a clumsy sleight-of-hand.

It is true that the supplanting of the traditional cosmology was less consciously dishonest than the atheistic doctor's rhetorical fraud. It was based more on genuine confusion than deliberate deception, but the effect was much the same.

With the increasingly materialistic consciousness of the modern world, it was rapidly forgotten that the study of the cosmos could ever have been about anything *but* physical matter. It was assumed that traditional science was trying to do the same things as modern science, but doing them badly. It was no longer recognized that the ancient wisdom has aims altogether different from those of material science, and that even when it superficially appears to be, it is not actually studying the same things.[1]

It is true also that most of the ancients did imagine the physical cosmos to be much the same as the metaphysical—that is, they failed to draw sufficient distinction between the subtle structure of the cosmos and its outward physical symbols. It is also true that they knew a lot less about the practical details of the *physical*

---

1. It should be borne in mind—especially in view of the traditional centrality of the Supernal Sun, or Solar Mother, which we shall encounter throughout this book—that the heliocentric (sun-centered) view of the cosmos also corresponds to a very apparent metaphysical symbolism. Indeed, geocentricity (earth-centeredness) is only valid from an earthly perspective. Dante is following tradition when he teaches that from the Heavenly perspective (or, in Platonic terms, in the Intelligible rather than the sensible cosmos) the earth (or material plane) is no longer the center, but the outer rim of being. And there are metaphysical reasons

universe than does modern science. Both these deficiencies are due to the fact that the purely physical level of being was not of very much interest to them and their main concern was with the higher truths that the phenomena of the material world symbolize.

It is natural for a culture to be relatively ignorant of the things it considers unimportant. If the ancient world was deficient in questions of material physics and astronomy, the modern world is at least equally ignorant in the areas of metaphysics and spiritual truth.

*

It is important to understand that our perception of the universe is mediated through the five physical senses. In theory, those five senses could be multiplied many times over. There is no limit to the number of senses we might, in principle, possess. It follows, therefore, that the portion of the cosmos prehensible to those five senses is only a tiny portion of total reality. If our senses were multiplied, we should be blasted by the terrifying immensity of the Universe: overwhelmed, crushed, and shattered by a multi-dimensional vastness too terrible for us to tolerate. "Human kind cannot bear very much reality."[2]

This little safe and sealed portion of the cosmos that has been allotted to us—this world of the five senses—is in itself an act of mercy, a manifestation of the kindness of our Great Mother. Goodness and kindness are woven into the very fabric of the cosmos, and

---

that the very lowest perspective—that of modern materialism—should reflect (within its own limitations) the very highest.

Copernicus, in arguing for a heliocentric cosmos, was putting forward an essentially theological or metaphysical view based on a Renaissance revival of the philosophic Solar Theism of the Classical world. He was by no means the prototype of the material scientist that modern popular mythology has attempted to make of him. Nor did he for one moment suppose that he was putting forward something new, but cited authoritative references from the ancient world for the heliocentric view. It is one of the ironies of history that his work should have served ends so far from his intentions, and in breaking down the traditional view of the cosmos, should have paved the way for the very antithesis of all that he believed in. A century later, the Church could only reply to the rising tide of cosmic demythologization with a short-lived attempt to suppress heliocentrism, for it (and Europe as a whole) had lost the intellectual foundation necessary to integrate it into the spiritual economy of the West.

2. T. S. Eliot, *The Four Quartets*: "Burnt Norton".

Nietzsche's vision of an empty, cold, meaningless universe is a foolish rejection of that goodness based on a profound misunderstanding of our place within the nature of things.

Imagine a tiny creature who spends her entire life on a table in a room. The surface of that table is a map of the world. The table, and indeed the whole room, represents the world of the five senses. This creature was taught from the beginning that the map on the surface of the table is a picture of the world, and that by studying it she may know the world and herself. Now imagine that one day this creature forgets the original tradition and decides to learn more than the map shows her. She makes telescopes and other instruments and soon she finds that she can see to the far ends of the room. She learns many things that were not included on her map of the world. She learns about tables and chairs, about the carpet and even, in the far distance, sees the window and the door, though she cannot quite be sure what they are.

Now she scorns her map and believes that she knows far more about the world than her credulous ancestors who believed in it. She has discovered countless things they never dreamed of.

But what *she* does not know is that beyond this room are other rooms, beyond all those rooms another house and then dozens of other houses in the same street and hundreds of other streets in the town, hundreds of other towns in the country, and hundreds of other countries in the world—and not only countries, but vast seas, forests, deserts, Arctic regions, underground caves, and inconceivably more. And all these things are shown on the map on the surface of the table; the map that she now believes to be 'obsolete' because of her new and superior knowledge gained by looking round the single room of that portion of the universe visible to the five senses.

Certainly she knows some things unknown to her ancestors, but they are a quite random assortment of things—just the things that happen to be in that particular room; and of those only the ones that are near enough for her to see clearly. They make no particular sense, of course, because they *are* a random selection, and so begins the Nietzschean vision—the assumption that, because the limited selection of reality available to our five senses is random, so the universe itself is meaningless and without pattern.

This Nietzschean vision, when faced squarely by a mind as courageous as Nietzsche's, does have something of the vast, terrifying quality of the vision we should see if our senses were multiplied to the point where we could see everything. Nietzsche himself went mad and ended his days in an asylum. Most lesser minds remain sane because they do not really face up to the full implications of what they believe.

Nevertheless, this vision is not—not remotely—the experience we should have if the kindly limitations of the world of the five senses were stripped away from us and we could see the totality of the cosmos in all its vicissitudes rather than that tiny compartment of it which is the physical world. Nietzsche and all those who believe that modern science has shown us "the universe as it is", are still living on the charity of our Great Mother; still resting in the enclosing protection of Her hand, shielded from the real Universe as It Is, the least glimpse of which would destroy them. Even as they boast of their rejection of tradition and ridicule the ancient map that She provided for us, they still live on the same table, in the same room in the same warm, comfortable house, sheltered from the terrible winds of the total cosmos.

But why is it not possible for us to see the total cosmos? Precisely because in our present state we are too weak to see it. Maid has the capacity to see the Whole; that is, to see the Absolute and the Infinite—to see the Divine, in which the total cosmos has its being. But seeing the Divine is precisely what humanity—and our present phase of humanity more than ever before—has strayed from. Opening us up to the total cosmos now would be to expose us to a massive overload of contingency—something like the Nietzschean universe multiplied countless millions of millions of times: an endless multi-dimensional chaos from which our souls could find no protection.

This is not because the universe *is* chaos, but because seen by one who had not attained true spiritual realization, it would necessarily *appear* so.

This gentle, protected, three-dimensional world is both a shelter and a school provided for us by universal Love. It gives us a safe world in which we may move closer to true spiritual realization and may also learn about the total cosmos in its true nature by studying the map that lies before us.

What is the map? In our little parable we know that the closed room is the universe prehensile to the five senses, but what exactly is the map? The map is the cosmos as presented directly to our unaided senses in this human life: the cosmos where the sun rises and sets, where the blue sky is a canopied dome above us, and where the seven planets move in their spheres—the Sun, the Moon, Venus, Jupiter, Mars, Mercury, and Saturn. As with every map, we need to know what its signs and symbols mean before we can read it properly, and this knowledge, or wisdom, has been handed down from the earliest times.

Similarly, we must interpret only what actually belongs to the map. It is no good trying to read meanings into fly-specks or ink-stains that may be on it. For example, modern science has 'discovered' three extra planets—Pluto, Neptune, and Uranus—and modern astrologers have incorporated them into their map of the cosmos. But these planets are not part of the immediately visible cosmos presented to us by Divine Providence.³ Nor are they really new discoveries. Certain ancient Sumerian seals, for example, depict the solar system with these extra planets, but Sumerian cosmology did not incorporate them into its fundamental world-picture.

Of course, it matters little what modern astronomers or astrologers do in this respect, since both have already lost the knowledge of the visible cosmos with its seven planets as an image of the totality of being, and both are unaware that what, from within the closed and protected world of the five senses, appears to be simply another star called the Sun is actually Divine Being itself seen through the 'covering' of the physical world.

It is not only in the dimension of space that the traditional and providential 'map' of the cosmos presents itself to us, but also in the dimension of time. And since an understanding of the traditional concept of time will enable us to acquire a firmer grasp of the entire subject, we shall now proceed to examine the traditional doctrine of the Cycles of History.

---

3. Though these 'outer planets' do possess a significance related precisely to those tenebrous influences that lie outside or beneath our cosmos (see note, p.83). Insofar as such influences begin to pervade the human sphere in the Dark Age, these planets may play a rather dubious rôle in terrestrial astrology.

Chapter Two

THE CYCLES OF TIME

THE TRADITIONAL picture of the cosmos not only views the things that surround us in space in a way radically different from that of the modern world, it also has a fundamentally different concept of time and the events that take place therein.

The modern world sees time as a straight line, and, despite increasing misgivings about whether a 'progress' is really taking place, is nonetheless bound by its own *mythos* to see history as essentially a process of progress or evolution.

The traditional view, on the other hand, no matter where we encounter it—in India or Europe, among the American Indians or the Australian Aborigines—regards the highest point of time as being the beginning, the Golden Age, the Garden of Eden, the Australian shamanic Dreamtime, or the simple "once upon a time" of our folk-tale traditions.

All of them recollect that the earliest times were the times when maid was closest to her divine origins, and all of them teach that as history moves forward, we necessarily move further and further from our celestial Point of Origin.

The history of language, among many other things, indicates that the traditional view is the correct one. If the modern, evolutionist point of view was correct, then we should expect languages to become simpler, less subtle, less complex, and less intelligent as we look further back.

What we find is, of course, the opposite. Anyone who has studied Latin or Greek knows how much more complex those languages are than their modern counterparts; how much more information is contained in a single word. Anyone who compares Latin with the modern dialects based on it—Italian, say, or French—can quickly see that the language has become vastly simplified and scaled-down for the sake of a less intellectual age. The same is true if we compare ancient Greek to modern Greek, or Sanskrit to Hindi.

Older languages contain far more words for the same things, expressing many subtle shades of difference that are largely lost to us.

People may ask: "Did the ancient Greek potter or serving-girl really work out all those case-endings and grammatical complexities in her head every time she opened her mouth? Could she have been intellectually capable of it?" The answer is: certainly, since she spoke no other language—but her descendants did not possess the same capacity, and as the generations went on, the language became adapted to less gifted intellects.

Language is the instrument and the mirror of our thought. People who spoke subtle and complex languages had subtle and complex thoughts. Modern languages grow ever more adept at discussing outward, physical things; ever less capable of expressing spiritual and metaphysical realities.

It is also noteworthy that the astonishing range of consonantal sounds in ancient languages makes it certain that maid's powers of both hearing and enunciation must have been far more accurate and finely tuned than our own; this is also confirmed by the study of ancient music with its remarkable subtlety of rhythm and melody.

Many things fall into place once we understand that the stream of time, like every natural stream, runs in the other direction from the one the modern world imagines—from the higher to the lower.

The ancient traditions divide the great Historical Cycle into four Ages. The Hindus call them the Sattwa Yuga, the Treta Yuga, the Devpara Yuga, and the Kali Yuga. In the West, they are called the Age of Gold, the Age of Silver, the Age of Bronze, and the Age of Iron. These ages are not of equal duration, but proceed according to the traditional figure called the Tetraktys, which divides the cyclic number ten into four in the ratio 4:3:2:1. So the last Age, our present Iron Age or Kali Yuga, represents only one-tenth of the entire Cycle.

The Iron Age is, according to traditional calculations, already over 6,000 years old, which leads also to the consideration that the whole period of patriarchal civilization has taken place within the Iron Age; and indeed, not even the whole of the Iron Age has been patriarchal.

The Golden Age is everywhere held to be the highest and best of the Ages, while the Iron Age is the darkest, characterized by discord and war, chaos and disorder. But what is the real, underlying difference between the Ages? What is the real nature of the Pattern of History?

The movement of history is essentially that of manifestation or materialization: from Spirit to matter, from inward to outward, and also—by the same token—from feminine to masculine. That this is the result of a cosmic cyclical movement rather than a mere 'historical accident' is evidenced, *inter alia,* by the fact that patriarchy supervened throughout the world, even in cultures that had no contact with each other.

In the earliest Age, maid was a much less physical being than she is now, and the world about her was also less physical. Many subtle influences existed and had far more power than they now have; it was upon the subtle domain that the eyes and heart of maid were concentrated, and there that her achievements lay. Physical things, insofar as they impinged on her at all, were valued primarily as symbols of higher and subtler things. As we shall see later, the knowledge that all material things are first and foremost symbols was not lost until very late in history.

The history of the world in the current Cycle (or in any Cycle) is essentially the history of consolidation or materialization. This is why there are few material remains of the very earliest part of the present Cycle. At that time maid might be said hardly to have touched the earth, and at first she was not physically manifest in matter at all. It is true that there are clear evidences of human civilization going back many millions of years—long before modern science imagines maidenkind to have 'evolved'—but clearly these evidences must relate to previous historical cycles.

Similarly, 'mythological' creatures, which modern science considers non-existent because of the lack of material remains, are often in fact creatures of a subtler level of being, which, never having been physically manifest, cannot possibly have left such remains, and with which maid increasingly lost the possibility of connexion as her own life descended progressively into the material realm to the exclusion of other possibilities.

*

From the matriarchal perspective—which is the original human perspective—femininity corresponds to the spiritual and qualitative pole of existence, and masculinity to the material and quantitative pole. From this it is clear that, as the historical cycle proceeds downwards into ever greater consolidation and materialization, and as maid herself becomes increasingly involved and preoccupied with matter, the masculine principle will become increasingly important at the expense of the feminine principle.

We can see this taking place even in matriarchal times. In the earliest eras of which we have evidence, going back at least 25,000 years, the statues are all of female figures. In later periods, male figures appear occasionally. After about 9000 B.C., male figures appear with increasing frequency, but always in a clearly subsidiary rôle; and it is not until some thousands of years after this that the first evidences of masculine predominance begin to make their appearance. Last of all do we see exclusively male religions such as Judaism, Christianity and Islam, which return to the very earliest one-sex form, but the other way about.

It is also important to note that when male figures first make their appearance, and for a very long time afterwards, the division between male and female divinities would seem to be as between Sky Mother and Earth Father, Sun Goddess and Moon God,[1] etc. In other words, those symbols associated metaphysically with the Spiritual are feminine, and those associated with the material are masculine. Much later, patriarchal societies reversed this symbolism, though, in many areas the more ancient correspondences remain in currency. For example, the Germans still refer to Frau Sonne (Madame Sun) and Herr Mond (Mr. Moon) and the Japanese still revere the Sun Goddess as ultimate ancestress of the Emperor. Countless other Sun Goddesses may be cited, from Lithuania to Ireland. The title Queen of Heaven was one of the commonest given to the feminine Deity, and while Jeremiah castigated the Hebrews for reverting to the worship of the Queen of Heaven, the Christians partially returned to Her fold, giving the same title to the Virgin Mary.

---

1. This certainly does not mean that the feminine civilizations lacked the beautiful concept of lunar femininity. The masculinity of the moon is only relevant from certain perspectives concerning the relation of the feminine and masculine principles. Feminine civilizations spoke of the Solar Mother and the Lunar Daughter. They also spoke of the lunarity of maid as compared to the solarity of God Herself. In this latter connexion, maid may be seen as the middle term of the triplicity Sun-Moon-Earth, being the mediatrix between Dea and the world.

Nevertheless, the great project of early patriarchy was to invert the normal correspondences of masculinity and femininity; to attribute masculinity to Heaven, the Sun and the Spirit; femininity to the earth, the moon and the material realm (a process known to archaeologists, with engagingly frank male-centeredness, as 'solarization').

It is interesting to note that 'feminists' who have from time to time attempted to revive a cult of the Earth Mother are in fact uncritically adopting the patriarchal point of view.

*

But despite the attempted reversal of symbols, the change from a feminine to a masculine orientation of society was necessarily accompanied by a steady and continuing descent into materialism and material preoccupations. Such a descent is, indeed, in the very nature of the historical cycle, and is the underlying reason for the change from a feminine to a masculine society.

Nonetheless, just as this transition was gradual, so the transition of the orientation of a civilization from spirit to matter was even more gradual.

All patriarchal civilizations continued to revere the spiritual traditions passed down from the earliest times, even if they made some changes in their outward forms.

During the early years of patriarchy, many new developments took place, all connected with continuing consolidation or materialization.

In many places the spiritual traditions and myths were written down for the first time. This would certainly not have been considered an 'advance' by the earlier feminine civilizations, which believed that only a thing known by heart was truly known; but certainly the 'solidification' of traditions in the fixed and material form of written tablets or papyri was becoming increasingly a necessity as the human mind grew weaker.

In many areas the Primordial Tradition was subject to new adaptations. Indeed, as the historical cycle continues downward, certain definite points are encountered at which radical changes take place throughout much of humanity. One such point occurred in the sixth century before the Christian era, when re-adaptations took place in many different civilizations at about the same time. In

China, the Single Tradition was divided into two separate parts: Taoism, which became the province of a spiritual élite and comprised the 'inner' doctrine, and Confucianism, which was of general social application. In Persia adaptations were made in the Mazdaean tradition by Zoroaster; in India Buddhism makes its appearance. For the Jews this was the period of the Babylonian captivity wherein many changes were made to the tradition. The same period begins the 'historical' period of Rome, after the 'legendary' era of the kings, and it is also known that highly significant changes were made among the Celts.

However, the most significant development of this period, from the point of view of things that were to follow much later, took place in Greece, where what is termed the 'Classical' period begins. This was characterized by an increasing 'humanism'—a breach with the Primordial Tradition and its spirituality. This involved an excessive cult of the reason as opposed to the Intellect or Solar Intuition (though certainly not so complete as to be comparable to the later 'rationalism' of modern Europe), and a concentration on material things in and for themselves rather than in the light of the higher things they symbolized.

While this is noteworthy in the Greek philosophy of this period, it is perhaps even more apparent in the art. The art of all traditional peoples, even up to the present, consists of an attempt not to depict the worldly and physical forms of things, but to draw the Archetypes or Celestial Forms that lie behind them. A century ago it was common to deride traditional art, whether found in modern India or in 'Palaeolithic' cave paintings, as being 'ignorant' of the laws of perspective, anatomy, etc. Now that these paintings are better understood, they are widely admired, and it is known that they were created according to laws quite other than those of anatomy or perspective, which are used to give the illusion of physical objects or beings. They spoke an artistic 'language' designed to reveal the symbolic and spiritual meaning of earthly things.

Plato was fully aware of this when he criticized contemporary Greek artists for making "copies of copies"—that is, for trying to draw an imitation of the physical man or the physical tree, which is itself only a symbol or 'copy' of a higher reality.

Plato, the greatest philosopher of the 'Classical' era, spent his life arguing against the errors of the new humanism and its breach with the Primordial Tradition, and teaching the fundamental truths of that Tradition, as did his master Socrates. For nothing could be more wrong, or more typical of the 'individualist' errors of the modern world, than to see Plato and Socrates as 'individual thinkers' with 'ideas of their own'. What they were in fact doing was to crystallize and adapt to the needs of their own spiritually troubled time (and hence of the times that followed them) the primordial and timeless wisdom in its specifically Indo-European form, closely akin to Vedic, Celtic, Teutonic, and Persian traditions.

Nonetheless, as is quite evident, Classical art continued to imitate the material world, creating anatomically perfect sculptures and developing an ever-greater faithfulness to material manifestation. Only with the decline of the Roman Empire and the waning of the Classical era did Western art return to the older aim of depicting the underlying spiritual reality; and it did this under the influence of a Christian philosophy deeply versed in Platonism.

*

The beginning of what is termed the 'modern period' is well known to be the European Renaissance. The Renaissance (meaning 'rebirth') was conceived as a rebirth of the Classical spirit, and in many respects it was precisely that. After a period during which the traditional spirit (in its patriarchal form, of course) had returned to the Western world, a reversion was consciously made to the artistic and philosophical principles of the Classical world, and the term 'humanism' was for the first time explicitly used, implying an outlook centered purely on the human domain and largely ignoring, if not yet actually denying, all that lay beyond it.

The restoration of Classical civilization was, of course, very in-complete, for the Classical world contained much inner depth of which the Renaissance imitator was unaware. There was at this time some revival of the traditional sciences—that is to say, those sciences based on the inner and metaphysical nature of things—of the West, but in the barren soil of a 'humanist' society they quickly perished, and soon the word 'science' was reserved exclusively for purely material studies of the material world. The entire scope of the new 'modern' culture became rapidly limited to the domain of the human individual and increasingly closed to all things higher or subtler.

Nevertheless, it is not true to say that the thread of the Primordial Tradition was entirely broken at this point, any more than it had been broken in the Classical period. There was, it is true, a very radical disruption; a change in the whole orientation of society, the creation of a form of civilization that, although prefigured in the Classical, had never been seen on the face of the earth before: that is, a civilization whose aims and preoccupations and *raison d'être* lay wholly in the human and material sphere. All previous civilizations and all contemporary civilizations, whether in India, China, Africa, or the Americas, took it for granted that the things of this world were but the reflections of higher things, and that the purpose of human life lay beyond human life itself. The modern civilization was the first civilization ever to restrict itself in principle to a purely worldly orientation.

But, as we have said, the thread of the Primordial Tradition was not yet entirely broken, and was not to be broken for a considerable time to come. This was partly because Western civilization remained nominally Christian. Even though the deeper significance of Christianity was largely forgotten, and the religion reduced to a primarily moral and personal affair, the thread connecting the human world with the divine was still there.

Again, even more significantly, the things of the world were still unconsciously seen, in many respects, as divine Essences. This deep intuition was not finally ruptured until the late nineteenth century, and even then the last thread of the Primordial Tradition was not broken for many decades.

*

It will readily be appreciated that the results of the Renaissance and of the 'modern' civilization that followed it were by no means uniformly 'bad'. It is usual to speak of the advances in medicine during this period, and while such a medicine was not necessary in earlier ages when subtler methods of healing were not forgotten and were fully effective, they had certainly been urgently required for many centuries. Again, we may speak of the findings of modern 'science', which, while certainly very restricted in its limitation to the material plane only, and unable to give any satisfactory account of the true meaning of things, nonetheless explored many facts that were undoubtedly true at their own material level, and one might say that the unfolding of the historical cycle would have been incomplete without them. Nor should one ignore the devastating effectiveness of this science when applied in a technical manner to the manipulation of the physical world. It is surely this aspect, most typical of a highly 'materialized' age and of one dominated by the masculine principle, which has done most to dazzle the multitude and to foster the illusion of a Universal Progress, of the superiority of the modern West to all other modes of civilization and the superiority of its knowledge to all other forms of wisdom.

While the reader of this book is scarcely likely to fall prey to this illusion, the progress of modern science and technics is certainly perfectly real and even admirable on its own level (leaving aside the many problems caused by its unrestrained exploitation in the absence of the controls that would have been imposed by a higher wisdom), and certainly constitutes one of the 'fruits' of the cycle that must necessarily be borne before it end.

On the cultural plane it must also be recognized that the work of a Michelangelo, or a Beethoven, of a Shakespeare, or of the English Romantic poets is very far from contemptible, nor are they devoid of spiritual qualities.

It is important to understand that none of these works could have come about in a fully traditional civilization. The 'naturalism' of Michelangelo (making copies of copies), the individualism and the 'personal-psychological' nature of Beethoven and the English Romantics all belong necessarily to an era formed by 'humanism'. Like modern science they are the realization of possibilities that belong to a distinctly inferior domain as compared to the spiritual arts of fully traditional civilizations; nevertheless, they are very wonderful and beautiful developments of their own kind, and all beauty partakes of the Primordial Beauty, is a portion or reflection of the Absolute Beauty of the Divine. If these particular beauties lay immanent within the current historical cycle, then it was necessary that they be expressed and manifested during its course; and by their very nature, that manifestation could only take place toward the end of its course. They are the winter-fruits of the historical cycle.

One might, of course, name countless other such winter-fruits in the cultural tradition that developed between the Renaissance and the cultural Eclipse of the 1960s.

For the 1960s mark another great turning point in the Cycle. Or, to be more accurate, they *may* mark another great turning-point. Alternatively, they may mark only the beginning of a relatively brief and temporary aberration in the course of history, such as we have witnessed on various occasions in the past. From our position of closeness to the events it is impossible as yet to be sure.

*

Whether it constitutes a new direction—in essence the beginning of the end of the historical cycle, and therefore of the world as we know it—or whether it is merely an aberration, it is necessary to understand that a very radical change took place in the 1960s, one that cannot be regarded as a simple continuation of what had gone before.

Up until that point, as we have said, the thread that connected Western humanity with the Primordial tradition, though stretched very thin, was not yet broken. In most of the fundamental intuitions of human life the West remained unchanged. It had lost a great deal of what it had formerly possessed, but these losses were an unavoidable part of the decline of the Cycle, and indeed were necessary in order for the modern world to realize its particular achievements.

What began in the 1960s was not so much a loss as an inversion. All the normal values of civilization were stood on their heads over a period of about twenty years, so that a person falling asleep in a public place in, say, 1955, and awakening thirty or forty years later would immediately think that she was in a world gone utterly insane. And she would be right. It is those who have become inured to the inversion, and have been persuaded by gradual inculcation and repetitive propaganda into accepting the post-Eclipse world as sane, who are mistaken.

In almost every sound instinct natural to a normal person and a normal civilization, the post-Eclipse world has effected a complete inversion. As we have written elsewhere:

"After the Eclipse, Western society went mad. It was a society stood on its head. All its values were inverted. The things sane societies loved, it hated; the things sane societies hated, it loved. The things sane societies tried to do, it tried to avoid; the things sane societies tried to avoid, it did with relish. It pursued chaos and hated order; it worshipped ugliness and loathed beauty. If sane people wished to dress as neatly and well as they could, these people were persuaded to dress as hideously and grotesquely as possible; if sane people wanted music to be melodious, these people (whether we are speaking of their 'popular' or their 'serious' music) were cozened into believing they liked raucous and tuneless noise. If women had been feminine, if home life had been secure, if children had been innocent, if men had been gallant, if art had been beautiful, if love had been romantic, then all these things must be stood on their heads. Of course, normal life before the Eclipse was not always like that. Of course, things had often fallen short of their ideals, or even of their minimal norms; but at least most people *tried* to do things properly and at least the surrounding civilization encouraged them to try. Never before had the deliberate *aim* been an inverted parody of all that should be. Everywhere after the Eclipse, in every area of life, a single principle reigned: inversion; the worship of chaos; the creed of the madhouse."

This process was not entirely new. Its principles had already been prefigured in the sphere of the visual and other arts. The visual arts often manifest the first signs of significant changes in a civilization, as was the case with the Renaissance itself. As we have already noted, the salient characteristic of traditional art, in all cultures throughout the world, is that it seeks to depict not the physical shadows of things, but the spiritual Realities that lie behind material things and are their very Essence. Post-Renaissance art was content to make "copies of copies", merely representing material things as they appear on the earthly plane; and because the things of the earthly plane are the symbols and shadows of higher Realities, such an art, insofar as it was faithful, could not help having a beneficent effect and a spiritual value of its own. In the twentieth century a new style of art appeared—under a variety of names: Surrealism, Cubism, Dada—that was no longer naturalistic; no longer sought to depict the physical things of the material world. But it by no means represented a return to the Primordial ideal of representing the spiritual truth behind those things; rather it plunged below the material level into the chaotic abysses of the inferior psychic domain.

While this took place in the sphere of 'high' art, it was certainly damaging, but its effects were by no means far-reaching. What happened during the 1960s was a massive explosion of this inferior psychism, with its grotesque inversion of values, into the life of the community as a whole. This was led in part by another visual movement, 'Pop Art', which was a kind of predigested surrealism for the masses, mixed with 'psychedelia'—the results of further delvings into the morbid chaos of the inferior psychic realm under the influence of hallucinogenic drugs. This consciousness was promulgated in a variety of ways through all the mass media of the time and especially through its popular music, rapidly perverting and inverting every area of human consciousness.

Just as in art we must now distinguish three essential stages: the traditional stage, in which art imitates spiritual Reality, the naturalistic stage in which art imitates nature, and the inverted stage in which art plunges into the inferior psychic domain, so we must also distinguish three distinct phases of civilization: the *Traditional Society* in which human life is oriented toward spiritual Reality, the *Normal Society* in which, while the deeper significance of life is largely forgotten, the love of beauty and goodness still governs human ideals, and the *Inverted Society* in which normal human bonds and loyalties are broken down and normal human ideals are inverted.

Before the Renaissance, Western society, with all its faults, was still fundamentally a Traditional Society; between the Renaissance and the mid-seventeenth century it was transmuted from a

Traditional to a Normal Society; and between the early 1960s and the early 1980s it was transmuted again from a Normal to an Inverted Society.

Note the very different lengths of time taken by the two transmutations. This may be because time itself accelerates as we reach the rim of the wheel; events following one another with ever more frenetic rapidity. Or it may be because the second transition is not a fundamental historical shift—the beginning of the End—but only a temporary aberration that may yet be rectified.

Chapter Three

THE THREE GUNAS IN HISTORY

IN CONSIDERING the three types of society mentioned toward the end of our last chapter, it will be instructive to bear in mind the Hindu doctrine of the three *gunas* or cosmic tendencies.

This important aspect of traditional science has been preserved in its most explicit form to the present day in the Indian branch of Tradition.

The three gunas exist at every level throughout cosmic existence, and may be seen at work in all beings and phenomena.

The three gunas comprise: *Sattwa*, the *upward* tendency, which is conformity to the pure essence of being—light, knowledge and purity; *Rajas*, the *outward* tendency, which constitutes the natural urge toward expansion on any given plane of being; and *Tamas*, the *downward* tendency, which is darkness or ignorance. From the human point of view, Sattwa is that tendency which leads us to higher spiritual states, above our earthly, human condition; Rajas is that which urges us toward expansion on the worldly and human plane, while Tamas is that tendency which leads toward states *below* the human.[1]

We may readily see that the *Traditional* mode of society is oriented to states above the human and earthly. Every aspect of the life of a

---

1. This can best be understood in the light of the ancient cosmic symbolism of the Cross, found in all cultures. The upright beam of the cross is the World Axis or Divine Thread that links all worlds. The horizontal beam represents a particular world-system or plane of being. Maid is the Axial creature of our world-system. Thus, while animals, fairies, and other beings exist purely on the horizontal level, maid, being on the Axis, has the power of choice and may also move either upward or downward, transcending her earthly state or falling below it. Thus, while the three gunas operate in all creatures as part of the mechanism of manifestation, in the activities of maid they may also have a special and more fateful significance. It is this that we are considering throughout the course of this chapter. The reader should also note that wherever the terms *vertical* and *horizontal* are used throughout this book, they are used with reference to this symbolism: for the World Axis is also the Beam of the Light of Essence, which strikes and in-forms the horizontal plane of material manifestation.

Traditional Society is lived in the light of Heaven. Its art, as we have seen, strives to depict not the earthly shadows of things, but the celestial Archetypes that lie behind them. Its crafts are not mere means to the manufacture of physical commodities, but each craft is a spiritual path, each operation performed in accordance with a sacred symbolism. This is why the factory system and the 'industrial revolution' could not happen until the traditional form of society had disintegrated—not because earlier civilizations 'lacked the intelligence' to bring about such innovations, but precisely because they were *too* intelligent to attempt them. They realized that such changes, while they might bring benefits on the purely material level, would destroy the deeper purpose of the human crafts, both for the producer and the consumer. For the producer, as we have said, the craft was a spiritual path into which she was initiated—and this was true in Europe until the destruction of the guild system at the time of the Renaissance. Not for nothing were the techniques of a craft called its 'mysteries'. For the consumer, on the other hand, whether the object be a decorated clay pot, a bridge, a chariot, a house, or a garment, the symbolism of its construction and decoration was also a support for contemplation, constantly leading her heart upward beyond the confines of the purely material. Traditional manufacture had as its object "to serve body and soul together".

Similar comments could be made regarding every aspect of the life of a Traditional Society, which thus is directed primarily by Sattwa, the upward tendency.

When we come to the *Normal* form of society which followed upon the breakup of the integral spirituality of Traditional civilization, we see a social order directed almost exclusively to the aims and purposes of this world. It is true that 'religion' continues to be followed by most people, but the very concept of 'religion' in the modern sense is new. It refers to a particular and specialized department of life which is the *only* one now specifically oriented toward things beyond this world and beyond the human state. Everything that is *not* 'religion' is now wholly mundane.

In many respects the Normal Society allows for expansion in areas wherein it was not possible before. As we have said, the industrial revolution with its attendant development of 'technology' becomes possible only in a Normal Society, as does the unfolding of a purely material 'science'. And, as we have discussed in an earlier chapter, many things become possible in the sphere of the arts now that it is no longer oriented toward things that transcend this world. The purely human and physical plane, now seen as the sole sphere of artistic endeavor, may be explored and developed in ways that were not possible to an upward-directed people, and the tremendous *outward* thrust of such a society is the most notable characteristic of the Renaissance period—one thinks of the Elizabethan era in England—and continues to be the guiding principle throughout the Victorian Era and in the Great American Century, which we would date from the Civil War to the early 1960s.

Since earthly things *are* a reflection of Heavenly things, the Normal Society, directed by earthly, Rajasic tendencies, is by no means devoid of a spiritual dimension. Its great art often has a spiritual quality, though always (even when it is religious art) at second-hand rather than in the directly spiritual manner of the arts of Traditional civilizations. The pursuit of beauty, in whatever form, can never be other than the pursuit of the absolute Beauty of the Divine, for there is ultimately no other source of beauty. The love and development of all the good things of human life: the family, the home, the bonds of love, all these are things that reflect the Heavenly order. In many respects, the Normal Society, though limited and unambitious from a spiritual point of view, continues to tread, at least in shadow-form, the Way of Heaven. It makes possible the realization of many of the lower and more material possibilities of the Historical Cycle, and thus is doing what is necessary; and in many respects, doing it well. This is the nature of a society directed by the outward tendency of Rajas.

What then would we expect of a society directed by the *downward* tendency of Tamas? Surely it would invert all those aspects of the Rajasic, or Normal, Society that still point upwards and partake of Sattwa. Its art will no longer seek to embody beauty and harmony, but will deliberately conform itself to whatever is ugly, misshapen and grotesque. In dress, rather than seeking to be neat and attractive, people will prefer to be sloppy, unkempt, or ridiculous in appearance. Rather than the highest elements of society setting the tone and being emulated by everyone else, the tone will be set by the lowest classes, other people increasingly coming to speak and act like them. Rather than attempting to support and maintain family life and personal loyalty, the propaganda of a Tamasic, or Inverted, Society will deliberately seek to break down the family, promoting a cult of 'personal independence' which cuts each soul off from those about her in an atmosphere of mutual distrust; each one is isolated in the prison of induced selfishness.

These are the things we should expect of a Tamasic Society, oriented to darkness and seeking neither to raise us above the human state (as does a Sattwic, or Traditional, Society) or to develop to the full a healthy human normality (as does the Rajasic, or Normal, Society); but seeking in every way to drag human life down toward the infra-human—toward the grotesque and the monstrous, the miserable, the isolated, and the vainly grasping: toward the character of the demonic realms depicted in the lore of every traditional civilization.

These are the things we should expect, and these are the things we find in the *Inverted* civilization that has developed since the Eclipse or 'social revolution' of the 1960s.

Needless to say, we are not unaware that many of these manifestations were in evidence before the 1960s—the pursuit of the grotesque and 'shocking' in art, for example, was developed in certain circles early in the twentieth century—but these earlier manifestations were of strictly limited influence. What is important in the 1960s is that they became increasingly general and rapidly displaced the normal and healthy instincts of society as a whole. Beatniks may have dressed like ludicrous monstrosities in the 1950s, but within a decade or two after the Eclipse, ordinary people, including grandmothers, were doing so.

It is also interesting to note that, in the Rajasic, or Normal, Society, looking at things purely in its own terms, we may see many signs of a continuous material 'progress'. Education becomes increasingly widespread and effective. Adult literacy is virtually total, except among the ineducable, and we may chart its rise and spread from the late nineteenth century through to the 1950s.

Crime and violence drop off dramatically in Normal conditions. In the late Victorian era murders took place daily in London. By the 1950s the national murder rate for a whole year was in low double figures.

In the 1950s the sight of a beggar in the streets of England was virtually unknown and would have seemed a strange throwback to the Victorian era.

It is true that many of these evidences of 'progress' were in fact merely the elimination of evils created by other Rajasic 'progresses' such as the Industrial Revolution with its attendant development of a large, depressed urban proletariat. Nonetheless, by the standards of a purely Rajasic, materially oriented society, things were getting better and better. The benefits of Rajasic industrialism were being increased while its evils were being eliminated, and an observer in the 1950s might reasonably have expected (as most people did) that all these tendencies would continue in the same direction, and that society would become happier, more peaceful, and better educated as time went on.

It is now very clear that such was not the case, and that most of the rising curves on the social progress-graphs of the 1950s turned suddenly and sharply in the opposite direction in the 1960s and continued downward for the ensuing decades.

By the 1990s, adult illiteracy was widespread, and even among the 'educated' section of society, University lecturers freely admit that the average undergraduate cannot spell, knows very little grammar and in general is rather less capable of expressing herself on paper than the average shop-girl in the 1950s. Most people of humble birth are back to the state of literacy that would have been theirs in the Victorian era. Violent crime, of course, has soared since the Eclipse. Murder, which was a rarity in the 1950s, has returned to late-Victorian levels and is rapidly escalating far beyond them. Beggary has returned to the streets.

In short, much of the progress of the later stages of the Rajasic, or Normal, Society has been destroyed by the Tamasic, or Inverted, Society. But, of course, it is not true to say that the Victorian era has returned, for while many of the evils of that era may be returning, none of its good qualities are, and whatever may be the outward social losses of the post-Eclipse period, they are as nothing compared to the impoverishment of soul: the loss of human loyalties and human dignity; the eradication of beauty and innocence from every department of human existence; the destruction, in sum, of all the things that make life meaningful and worthwhile.

*

It is important to note that the periods of time occupied by the three types of civilization are very much incommensurate in length—much more so even than the four great Ages of the Historical Cycle, for the Traditional Society occupies almost all of the Historical Cycle, with the Normal Society only appearing briefly at the end, and the Inverted Society still more brief.

It is not, in fact, quite as simple as this. Normal societies—that is, outwardly directed Rajasic societies which have lost sight of the true upward aim of life—have existed at other periods of history. Ancient Rome is one example, although the Classical world was by no means so purely this-worldly and lacking in metaphysical underpinning as the post-'Enlightenment' period of the modern West. There have also been earlier eras in which the worldly direction of a Rajasic period would tend toward the psychic rather than the material domain, giving an excessive importance to sorcery (much more effective in less 'consolidated' periods of history) much as the modern world gives an excessive importance to 'technology'—and perhaps such phases of civilization made possible the realization of certain 'lesser fruits' of the Historical Cycle proper to their own time, even as the Normal Society recently deceased in the West has done in ours.

It is possible even that these ancient Rajasic eras tailed off into brief periods of Tamasic degeneration akin in some respects to the post-Eclipse period of our own time. One thinks, for example, of the madness and degeneracy of late Rome with its carnivals of slaughter and cruelty in the arena; and one cannot but be struck by a horrifying parallel in the increasingly explicit, near-pornographic depiction of violence, not only in fictional films but in television newsreels in the post-Eclipse world. It seems that at a certain stage in a Tamasic period, the thirst for death, carnage, and suffering as a public spectacle inevitably makes itself felt and demands satisfaction.

Nonetheless, Rajasic periods are to some extent aberrations within the normal course of the Historical Cycle, occupying, even when all are aggregated, a very small portion of the whole. Tamasic periods, being times of utter degeneration, and having no legitimate principle of existence whatever, necessarily represent a very much tinier proportion of the whole. By their very chaotic and unstable nature they cannot be more than the very briefest of interludes historically speaking.

Traditional, Sattwic societies are the historical norm, and the end of such Rajasic or Rajasic-Tamasic interludes as we have been discussing is generally a new revelation of Truth, or a new adaptation of an existing tradition to the consolidated conditions of a new era. One thinks of the Christian revelation coming at the end of the Classical period.

It is also to be noted that all three gunas are necessarily present in all worldly things. Even the Sattwic perfection of the Golden Age must have had some admixture of Rajas and Tamas, and as time goes on and the world becomes ever more 'consolidated', Rajasic and Tamasic elements become increasingly prominent. The patriarchal revolution of the early Iron Age is one result of this tendency, which obviously had become very marked by such a late stage of the Cycle.

*

Now similarly, we may divide the history of femininity into three stages, corresponding to the three gunas. These stages do not directly coincide with the three discussed above, except that the last, Tamasic stage also begins with the Eclipse. The first, and by far the longest, is the Sattwic stage of femininity, or what is called the 'matriarchal' period. This lasts for the whole of the first three Ages and for a small part of the Iron Age—in other words, for more than nine-tenths of the historical cycle. This is the period in which femininity is recognized as the highest principle both on earth and in the higher realms: as that principle which leads beyond this world to the higher levels of being. All evidence points toward the universality of the feminine principle in human art, society, and worship. Whether women were the material rulers of civilization we cannot say for certain. The ingrained prejudice of a masculine-dominated society reacts strongly against such an idea; but there is no reason why it should not have been so, and since in all known traditional societies there was a strong analogy between the earthly monarch and the Heavenly power, it seems overwhelmingly likely that such was the case.

Whether it was or not is, however, of relatively small importance. What *is* vital is the fact that femininity and the feminine image was clearly the supreme and governing *principle* of this vast period of human history—throughout the Golden Age, longest of the Ages, when human spirituality and intellectuality were at their highest; throughout the long decline of the Ages of Silver and Bronze, still periods immeasurably superior to our own; and even into the early years of the Iron Age itself. Femininity is the natural ideal of human civilization. Only by a very late revolution in the last, shortest, and most inferior Age did the cult of the superiority of the masculine become established.

A typical comment of the modern mind upon 'matriarchy' is to say that it must only have been patriarchy the other way round. But such is very far from being the case. As we shall see in a later chapter, femininity has very definite characteristics that are a part of the metaphysical nature of things. To say, for example, that if men are considered the active, forceful, even violent sex under patriarchy, women must have been considered the same way under matriarchy, is founded on a complete misunderstanding of the nature of femininity, both in its metaphysical essence and in its biological reflection on earth.

In a 'matriarchal' or, we had rather say, a feminine society, women as the leading and most revered sex are revered precisely for their feminine qualities, which do not change whether in feminine or masculine societies. They are always the 'passive' sex in the sense of being the one less oriented to outward activity, and in this, in feminine societies, they are assimilated to the Principle itself, which causes motion without itself moving. This is not to say that women did nothing, either in feminine or patriarchal societies, but that symbolically the qualities of serenity, peace, and contemplation are considered superior to dynamic outward activity. Or rather, the latter is said to depend upon and be always subordinate to the former.

This, indeed, is understood even in patriarchal societies, where, for example, in the Hindu Tantrik tradition the male principle (the god or *deva*) is considered to be the superior and therefore the serene, unmoving principle, while his female counterpart (or *shakti*) is his outward activity or energy. This is rather curious according to most later patriarchal thinking about the nature of femininity, just as it was to matriarchal thinking. But the reversal was necessary in order to preserve metaphysical truth and patriarchal doctrine at the same time. In Tibet, which remains closer to the original matriarchal tradition (polyandry was until recently practiced there), the position is reversed—that is to say, normal—and the serene Deity is female while her *shakti* or outward energy is male. Similarly, in Tibet, in the case of the complementary principles of Wisdom and Method—representing the Essential or Spiritual principle and the substantial or material respectively—Wisdom is female and Method male.

The Hindu Tantrik tradition notwithstanding, in general patriarchy has not attempted to alter the relative qualities of masculinity and femininity. Rather it has revalued them in metaphysical terms, associating feminine serenity with the passivity of matter and male activity with the relatively 'active' power of the in-forming Spirit or Essence. And, insofar as patriarchy is a legitimate tradition, albeit one belonging purely to the inferior state of the Iron Age, this can be accepted as one of the permissible permutations of the expression of Truth.

Nonetheless, throughout the patriarchal period, the feminine continually shines through in its true glory, despite all ideological opposition. From the great Goddesses of various traditions, who so often overwhelm their appointed Gods in the hearts and souls of the people, to the Blessed Virgin Mary, who rapidly adopts the titles of Supreme Deity—Seat of Wisdom, Rose of the World, Queen of Heaven.

The worship of femininity breaks through again and again—for example, in the chivalry of the Middle Ages, so ignorantly dismissed by modern people as a "subterfuge for the suppression of women" (as if such subterfuges were in any way necessary!) but which was in fact nothing short of a spiritual cult of the feminine image.

This, then, was the second, or Rajasic, age of femininity, much shorter than the first, or Sattwic, age. Instead of being exalted, as in the Sattwic age, femininity is pulled this way and that: sometimes vilified, sometimes revered, but always recognized for what it is, always kept alive by the very nature of woman herself and by the inherent beauty and divinity of the feminine principle.

Once again we must ask, since we understand the Sattwic and the Rajasic ages of femininity, what should we expect to occur in its Tamasic age? Surely we should expect the eclipse of femininity itself—the banishment of the feminine principle from the earth as far as such a thing is possible. In the Sattwic age femininity is exalted. In the Rajasic age it is buffeted this way and that, but remains always essentially itself. In the Tamasic age it must be darkened, obscured, and even destroyed.

And what do we see after the Eclipse of the 1960s? Precisely that. Femininity is not only trivialized and despised, but its very existence is denied. According to the 'official' dogma of the post-Eclipse world, femininity is nothing but the product of 'social conditioning'. It is something to be thrown off by modern women as a vestige of a superstitious past. Women are trained to think like men, talk like men, act like men, and dress like men; to have the same ambitions and exteriorist preoccupations. They are trained to regard femininity as weakness, and conformity to the masculine model as 'liberation'. They are trained to regard masculine values as right and normal, and feminine values as something to be avoided, something—most ironic of all absurdities!—invented by men for their oppression.

The post-Eclipse world has seen, in a few short decades, the ultimate triumph of patriarchy, something not dreamed of by the ultra-patriarchal ancient Athenians or by any of the most extreme masculinists of history. The post-Eclipse world has seen the complete destruction of femininity and its extirpation from the one place that would have seemed its safest haven and ultimate sanctuary—from the soul of woman herself.

And for the first time in history, we inhabit a world where femininity is dead: a harsh, barren, totally masculine world.

Chapter Four

THE NATURE OF FEMININITY AND THE NATURE OF BEAUTY

Modern science especially ignores what the ancients denoted by the name of 'form', precisely because here there is a question of a non-quantitative aspect of things, and such ignoring is not unrelated to the fact that this science discerns no criterion in the beauty or ugliness of a phenomenon. The beauty of a thing is the sign of its internal unity, its conformity to an indivisible essence, and therefore to a reality that can neither be counted nor measured.

TITUS BURCKHARDT

FEMININITY has always been recognized as one of the fundamental Essences or Archetypes of the human world. And not only of the human world: for throughout most of our history—throughout all but the tiniest part of it—it has been recognized that what is true of humanity is also true of the cosmos.

The sun and moon existed long before the ball of gas and the ball of rock came into being that incarnate them outwardly for us. Numbers were before there were things to be numbered. And femininity existed long before any female creature came into existence.

For in each of these cases, we are speaking of primal Realities. Principles that cannot not be. Realities that may be manifested in different ways upon different levels of being, but which are not dependent on this or that manifestation for their actuality.

Of course, the doctrine of the post-Eclipse world is the precise reverse of this. It sees all ideals, all principles, all *intelligent* realities, as merely epiphenomena of the material world. In the case of femininity, it declares quite categorically that it does not exist. Femininity, we are told, is merely the result of social conditioning. Women are female in a purely bodily sense, but femininity—the *mental* and *spiritual* aspect of the female phenomenon—is merely a product of social conditioning. Give a woman the same opportunities as a man, and she will do the same things, want the same things, and feel the same things as a man.

Yet even from the merely biological point of view this is demonstrably untrue. The female *brain* is physically very different from the male. This is caused not so much by genes as by hormones. The human brain is naturally inclined to be feminine. It is massive doses of the male hormone testosterone, both during gestation and at puberty, that make a male brain different from a female brain. If the brain is not bathed in testosterone at critical stages, a genetic male will not develop male mental characteristics. As an adult, even if he is anatomically male, a man may have a brain that remains female. It is also possible for a woman to have a male brain, but both these occurrences are very rare. In general, men have male brains and women have female ones; and this, in biological terms, is why men are masculine rather than merely male and women are feminine rather than merely female. It is not a matter of social conditioning. It is a matter of biology. To quote Dr. Anne Moir, who has made a voluminous compilation of the most recent scientific research on this subject: "Men are different from women... to maintain that they are the same in aptitude, skill, or behavior is to build a society based on a scientific and biological lie." It is also to rob women of their particular identity, which is their femininity.

To put it simply, in the female brain some mental functions are distributed around the left and right hemispheres of the brain, while in the male brain they are more compartmentalized. For example, the parts of a woman's brain that govern speech and emotion are spread across both halves, whereas in a man they are locked into discrete locations. Moreover, the corpus callosum, which connects the left and right brains, is thicker and more highly developed in women, so the two halves of the brain communicate better. In practical terms this means that women tend to be more verbally fluent than men, and their reason and emotion are more closely allied. Also, since they can bring more diverse parts of the brain to bear on a problem, they are better able than men to arrive at apparently non-rational but correct conclusions. 'Woman's intuition' has a biological aspect (although that is by no means all there is to it). Men, on the other hand, are better at mathematics, have better hand-eye coördination, and more easily grasp spatial relations. For every mathematically gifted girl there are thirteen mathematically gifted boys, and the best boys are always better than the best girls. Boys, however, are four times more likely to be in remedial reading classes than girls. These differences are fashionably attributed to 'social conditioning', but in fact they manifest from the earliest ages, long before social pressures could take effect. One researcher says: "After fifteen years looking for an environmental explanation and getting zero results, I gave up."

Some purely biological differences have been widely confirmed but are almost unknown outside the laboratory. A woman's senses, for example, are more acute than a man's. She can hear, taste, smell, and feel certain things he cannot, and she has better peripheral vision. In some sensory tests there is no overlap between the least sensitive woman and the most sensitive man.

A lot of important evidence comes from abnormal conditions. Certain medications and physiological conditions can produce abnormal flows of female hormones in a woman's body while she is pregnant. These hamper the flow of testosterone to the brain of a male child, producing effeminate men who may be (but are not necessarily) homosexual. Such men have brains that operate more like those of women. They use language better than other men and their mental functions are more distributed around the brain. Their senses are more acute than those of other men, though not as acute as those of women, but they have less mechanical ability. Effeminate men are less aggressive and less power-hungry than other men. These conditions have been reproduced in laboratory tests. Effeminate male rats are bred without fail by blocking the normal action of testosterone.

Equivalent effects have been found in women. Girls born with a genetic abnormality called Turner's Syndrome do not possess ovaries. Since ovaries produce a small amount of masculinizing testosterone, these girls do not have even a small check on the natural femininity of the brain. They are exaggeratedly feminine, shy, romantic, and sensitive. Their sense of mechanics and spatial relations is also exaggeratedly female; many have a difficult time remembering how to get to school. On the other hand, when girls in the womb are exposed to abnormal doses of testosterone the very opposite happens. They grow up as aggressive tomboys, with an interest in guns and trucks. Not surprisingly, they are likely to be better than most women at mathematics and mechanics.

The idea that 'social conditioning' has forced women to be feminine, that femininity is an artificial product of patriarchal ideology, could not be further from the known facts. Women are *naturally* feminine. When their biological femininity is exaggerated by hormone imbalances, they become exaggeratedly feminine in *precisely* the ways that femininity has always been 'conventionally' defined. When their biological femininity is hormonally deficient, they become deficient in precisely those 'conventional' feminine qualities. There can be no doubt that natural, biological femininity is precisely coincident with 'socially defined' femininity.

Women are not feminine because they are 'conditioned' into being so, but because they are *made* that way.[1]

We need hardly say, however, that we do not take the view that femininity is biological in origin. On the contrary, biology is merely a physical expression of something much profounder. It is no more than the material mechanics through which the eternal Form called Femininity is made manifest on earth. Just as the human body is the vehicle of the soul, so the female body—and the female brain—are the earthly vehicles of the Feminine Archetype. Just as the soul transcends the body, existing both before it and after it, so the Eternal Feminine transcends all female species existing both before they came into being and after they have passed away.

We have cited biological evidence mainly for the purpose of making it clear that *even on its own terms* the late-twentieth-century view of femininity is wrong. The ultra-patriarchal dogma that denies the existence of femininity and 'explains it away' as 'social conditioning' can only exist by ignoring not only the traditional metaphysical view held by all people at all times outside the modern West, but also by ignoring the very material 'science' upon which its view of the world claims to be founded.

Let us also note that this dismissal of femininity rests upon an almost ludicrously male-centered view of the world. Its essential

1. Post-mortem examinations of the brains of male-to-female transsexuals have revealed structural elements typical of female brains, indicating that even when social conditioning works in the *other* direction a female brain produces feminine behavior.

premise is that masculinity is the natural, normal, 'neutral' way for human beings to be, while femininity is something odd and unusual. Thus, in an ultra-patriarchal society, for women to wear trousers is considered perfectly normal and unexceptionable (unlike the equivalent of men wearing dresses). Masculine behavior, according to ultra-patriarchy, is *normal* behavior, acceptable—and, increasingly, quasi-compulsory—for all people. Thus femininity can be dismissed as an artificial product of 'social conditioning' precisely because its opposite, masculinity, is seen as the natural state of human existence. People, left to themselves, will behave the way men behave. Femininity is something that has to be learned. Yet the irony is, that even on the purely scientific, biological view (upon which the modern ideology pretends to base itself), the reverse is true. Human beings, and all creatures, are *naturally* feminine, some of them then becoming masculine through the action of male hormones.

However, these considerations are at most of secondary importance. What concerns us are the fundamental Realities, of which biological and social phenomena alike are but earthly reflections.

What then, from the Essential point of view, is femininity? This is a question that may be answered on many levels.

The feminine is traditionally symbolized by the sign of Venus and the masculine by the sign of Mars. Thus, at a relatively low level, we may see that while the masculine is concerned with discord and opposition, the feminine is concerned with concord and harmony. Patriarchal history has been marked by war (the fundamental meaning of Mars) and by violence. Commentators on the archaeological remains left by the most recent of the feminine civilizations—most notably that found in Crete—are continually struck by the absence of signs of warfare. In feminine Crete, a civilization with vast multi-storied palaces, villas, farmsteads, harbor installations, and advanced transportation, where the statues show the complete preponderance of the feminine image, the cities are not surrounded by walls and fortifications as they are in the various contemporary empires that were, by this time, already patriarchal. Frescoes of conquering kings, of severed arms and heads, abound in these patriarchal kingdoms, but in Crete, where sacred Queens commanded great wealth and power and lived in palaces more splendid than most of their royal male contemporaries, no sign of this sort of thing is to be found. Elsewhere, the city-states that lived side by side were in a state of perpetually changing war-alliances, sieges, and battles. In Crete, proud and powerful cities lived side by side in peace for many centuries.

Peace, in the sense of the simple absence of warfare, is however only a manifestation of a deeper principle—the principle of harmony or *bonding*, by which a society is bound together in a state of organic wholeness. The importance of this will become clearer in a later chapter as we examine the phenomenon of social *atomization* that characterizes the ultra-patriarchal society of the post-Eclipse world. For while discord may be a feature of all patriarchal societies when compared to feminine societies, we shall see that as the Tamasic stage of super-patriarchy sets in, discord reaches critical proportions, with all bonds and loyalties being corroded and each individual being atomized into a lonely, isolated unit trapped in the solitary confinement of an illusory 'personal independence'.

It is clear that the majority of patriarchal civilizations have been very far from this late state of atomization, but we may also see that even among some of the greatest of patriarchal minds atomized egocentricity plays an astonishingly prominent rôle. For example, the teachings of Plato and of Aristotle will be drawn upon in this work, not, as we have said, because those teachings originated with their authors (if they had they would be worthless for that very reason), but because they encapsulate the Eternal Wisdom in a form suited to the relatively limited understanding of the later days of the West. Platonic idealism and Aristotelian hylomorphism express two aspects of traditional ontology, and are both valuable and necessary as two sides of the same coin.

Nevertheless, Aristotle did not scruple to criticize his teacher Plato and even to claim to have refuted the doctrine of the Archetypes (which he must then reintroduce by the back door, since his own work makes no sense without it). Such foolishness is typical of the masculine approach to life. From the feminine perspective, philosophy is a pursuit of Truth; argument is a seeking and a clarification. From the masculine, all too often, it becomes a vehicle for the ego. That many patriarchal saints and sages have been above such egocentricity we freely and happily admit. But that one as great as Aristotle (and he is far from being an isolated example) should descend to such divisive egoism is in itself a startling indication of the atomizing tendency endemic in the patriarchal world.

*

Probably the most salient characteristic of femininity is beauty. Most languages term woman the Fair Sex, or some equivalent, and the very word 'beauty' sounds strange and outlandish when applied to a man.

According to the late-patriarchal materialist world-outlook, this attribute of femininity is considered a thing of the smallest possible importance. It is therefore vital to understand that even in the patriarchal West, beauty has normally been considered very far from trivial.

Plato uses *to kalon*, 'the beautiful', as a term expressing the Absolute, and in this he is at one with all tradition.

In order to understand this, we must realize that there is a very profound difference between the traditional understanding of beauty and the late-patriarchal concept.

The late-patriarchal world believes of beauty, as it does of femininity, that it does not really exist. That is, beauty is not for the late-patriarchal world an objective cosmic Reality. It is merely a 'matter of taste'. In other words there is no such thing as an objectively beautiful thing—only things that, being quite neutral in themselves, are merely *considered* beautiful by human beings.

Let us recall the quotation from Nietzsche with which we began. He tells us that in the universe:

> . . . *order, structure, form, beauty, wisdom, and whatever other human aesthetic notions we may have are lacking.*

"Human aesthetic notions". Mark that very important phrase. For Nietzsche—and he is speaking for the entire 'modern' point of view—beauty is a purely human construction. It begins and ends in our brains. It has no ultimate objective reality.

And note also that apart from *wisdom* (Sophia—also traditionally feminine), all of the terms Nietzsche uses are synonyms of beauty.

56

Order, structure, form: all are terms for the principle of form as opposed to formlessness, and therefore for the beautiful. The Greek word for order is *kosmos*—the term for the universe itself, as opposed to *chaos* (note how these very words imply a world-view based on the precise opposite of what Nietzsche is saying). And our word *cosmetic* comes from that same *kosmos*, because order and beauty are the same thing.

What Nietzsche is involuntarily demonstrating is that when we want to describe the natural, human view of the cosmos, even if only to repudiate it, we keep finding ourselves forced back on terms that mean *form* and *beauty*.

We shall discover that this is very important—indeed, quite central to a metaphysical understanding of the universe.

But for the moment let us pause and consider the possibility that beauty is not a relative human perception, but an objective reality. That, indeed, beauty is a cosmic reality that characterizes all sorts of different things—a flower, a star, a song, an angel—just as surely as hotness characterizes a sun and a fire, or wetness an ocean and a drop of dew.

We should be grateful if you would pause for just a moment in reading this page, and think about this most important concept—that beauty is a cosmic reality, not merely a human perception; that beauty is as objectively real as heat or light or weight. Because if, even for a moment, even partially, you can let this truth take hold of you, you will have broken one of the chains that bind you, and will have seen a glimpse of the cosmos as it really is.

We have said that beauty is as objectively real as heat or light or weight, and it is. But clearly there is an important difference between beauty and these other qualities. They are *quantitative* and beauty is *qualitative*. They can be weighed or measured. Beauty cannot. It is for this reason, of course, that the modern outlook denies the objective reality of beauty. From the modern point of view, only that is real which can be *quantified*.

From the traditional point of view, quantitative things are *less* real than qualitative things. Quantitative attributes possess only a relative reality. Qualitative attributes belong to the Absolute. A thing may be very hot or very heavy, but there is no such thing as absolute heat or absolute weight.[2]

On the other hand, there *is* such a thing as absolute Beauty. Absolute Beauty is that which characterizes the Divine. All earthly beauty is but a participation in this absolute beauty, and when we say that a thing is more beautiful or less beautiful, we do not mean it in a quantitative sense. Beauty cannot be measured. We mean that the thing in question participates to a greater or lesser degree in the absolute Beauty—reflects it more or less perfectly in its own kind.[3]

*

Now this distinction that we have drawn between qualitative and quantitative things is closely related to the distinction between the feminine and the masculine. Ultimately, femininity, with its salient characteristic of beauty, belongs to the qualitative pole of existence—to the pole of Essence or Form—while masculinity belongs to the quantitative pole, the pole of substance or matter.

All traditions agree that the fundamental movement of the Historical Cycle is from the qualitative to the quantitative pole: from the predominance of essence or form to the predominance of substance or matter.

Patriarchal traditions associate the qualitative or Essential pole with the masculine and the quantitative or substantial pole with the feminine. Feminine or 'matriarchal' traditions associate the Essential pole with the feminine and the substantial pole with the masculine.

---

2. Nonetheless, it should be remembered that all quantitative attributes are reflections of qualitative Realities. Light, for example, is always the earthly reflection of the Primordial Light (that light not seen with eyes); wetness is ultimately a partaking in the quality of Elemental Water, of which H_2O is only a shadow. In truth, quantitative things ultimately owe their whole existence to the qualitative Realities they mirror.

3. It is for this reason that the cultivation of beauty in our own lives is of fundamental importance, while the cultivation of ugliness or disorder in dress and personal appearance (as well as in art, design, and other spheres) is a dark ritual of the Tamasic period and must be resisted. It is sometimes asked: "What of those who have the misfortune to be personally unattractive?" But physical ill-favoredness is merely an accident of the world of flux. The plain maid who makes herself as neat and beautiful as she can be is acting in conformity with the Light. The well-favored maid who conforms to Tamasic fashions of ugliness and absurdity invokes the darkness.

Patriarchal traditions are, of course, only acting out the logic of their masculinized theology, and their interpretation makes sense within the economy of their particular outlook. Nonetheless, objectively, it is hard to deny that the feminine perspective is the correct one. The historical descent from Essence to substance, from Form to matter, has gone hand in hand with the historical movement from feminine to masculine civilizations; and the most purely quantitative form of civilization ever conceived—that of the post-Eclipse world—is also the era of super-patriarchy in which the feminine principle has been eradicated as far as possible from every area of human life, including the heart of woman herself.

From the perspective of the feminine metaphysics that has constituted human intellectuality for the vast majority of our history, the increasing dominance of the quantitative and substantial over the qualitative and essential must be seen as *one and the same phenomenon* with the increasing dominance of the masculine principle over the feminine. And historically speaking, there can be no doubt that this is precisely the case. We therefore make no apology for the fact that, for the rest of this book, we shall treat this question from the feminine perspective.

It may also be noted that, as the masculine principle reaches the completion of its triumph, patriarchal society itself no longer seeks to deny the traditional feminine perspective. The modern 'scientistic' outlook with its worship of the quantitative and its denial of the qualitative, is more than happy to associate the quantitative and substantial with masculinity. This, we may say, is the culmination of patriarchy—the *embrace* of the quantitative and the complete rejection of the qualitative. No longer is there any desire to invert the natural order and associate masculinity with the qualitative. This is what patriarchy becomes when it has lost every last trace of the spiritual heritage of its feminine mother-tradition.

We shall also see that the masculine tendency toward dispersion or atomization is ultimately the same thing as the masculine tendency toward quantity and substance.

It is now necessary to examine in greater detail the nature of these two fundamental principles: quality and quantity, or Essence and substance.

Chapter Five

THE KEY TO METAPHYSICS

IN SOME respects this is the most important chapter in the book. Our aim is to understand the most fundamental concept of traditional metaphysics. Once we have fully grasped this, everything else will begin to fall into place.

We call traditional thought *Essentialist*, because it is, by definition, that intellectuality which recognizes the universal Pole of Essence and (which is in fact the same thing) recognizes that all existing entities, from an ant to a galaxy, are what they are precisely because of their Essential forms or Archetypes.

The late-patriarchal ideology, which we may call *substantialist*, or *accidentalist*, in contradistinction to Essentialist, consists precisely and wholly in a denial of the Pole of Essence and of the Essences of entities. Everything else the modern world believes flows from this denial. The whole project of late-patriarchal thought is to explain the universe wholly in terms of matter or substance, and to deny Form or Essence.

At first these concepts may seem difficult. That is hardly surprising, since we are discussing things that lie completely outside the thinking of the modern world. Nevertheless, the Essentialist way of thought has been the underlying model for *all* human conceptualization from the Golden Age right through to the so-called Enlightenment of the seventeenth century, and Essentialism was only fully eradicated from the normal thinking of most educated people toward the end of the nineteenth century.

In truth, there are only, and can only be, *two* ways of thinking—the Essentialist and the substantialist. All the different philosophies, ideologies and outlooks of the modern world, from Marxism to the New Age movement to the 'ordinary common-sense outlook' of most people who believe they have no philosophy at all, are simply variations on the underlying theme of substantialism.

It is as difficult for a modern person to understand what substantialism is as it is for a fish to understand what water is. She has lived her whole life in a substantialist atmosphere, living, drinking, and breathing substantialism. She has learned physics, history, literature, and geography from the substantialist perspective, reads substantialist newspapers, and watches substantialist thriller films. Even when she reads the literature of past ages, she cannot help seeing it through the substantialist spectacles provided by her surrounding culture.

The only way to understand what substantialism is, is to step outside it. And that means seeing the world from the other perspective. The *only* other perspective. That of Essentialism.

Before we begin, let us anticipate one important question that is likely to arise in the mind of an intelligent reader. She may say, as we expound Essentialism: "But surely all the peoples of the world before the seventeenth century were not versed in this rather complex philosophy. Can we really say that this was the basis of all human thinking?" And our answer to this must be: "Has every modern person read the works of Descartes and Hobbes and Locke? Could she describe to us, even vaguely, the broad thrust of modern philosophy from the 'Enlightenment' to the present?" Of course she could not. Most people are not theorists. But nevertheless, every modern person is profoundly affected by this stream of thought. She is what she is, believes what she believes, and (more importantly) assumes what she assumes because of it. In watered-down, tenth- and twelfth-hand form, it constitutes the background to her entire view of the world.

So it is with the traditional person. Any given individual may or may not have been able to expound her fundamental philosophy as we are about to do. If she could, she would perhaps have expressed it rather differently. Nevertheless, what we are about to explore will give you a much clearer idea of what the traditional person thought and why she thought it. It will make clear not only the thought of the ancient and mediaeval worlds and of the many non-European civilizations, but it will also throw much light on works from Shakespeare to Keats and Wordsworth. Browning and Tennyson were probably the first truly great English poets to adopt unconsciously and almost completely the substantialist outlook.[1] Far more important,

---

1. Pope and Dryden and the 'classical' poets of the eighteenth century were certainly 'worldly' in their outlook, and the Romantic Movement was in some respects a healthy reaction against this. Nevertheless, their outlook was not

the following will make clear what Essentialism is, and how it is possible to think otherwise than in the terms laid down by the modern world.

*

The most fundamental concept of Essentialism is that the universe possesses two Poles. These two Poles may be illustrated as follows:

FORM	MATTER
ESSENCE	SUBSTANCE
QUALITY	QUANTITY
FEMININE	MASCULINE

Now these two Poles are absolutely essential to all manifestation whatever. Nothing can exist that is not a marriage of essence and substance, or of form and matter.

Let us say we have a statue of the Goddess Diana carved in marble. What is the Form or Essence of this statue? The shape of the Goddess. What is its substance? Marble. Now, suppose we could remove the Essence or Form from the statue. We should no longer have a statue of Diana. What should we have? Simply a piece of marble. Now, is this piece of marble pure substance or matter? Certainly not, because it still has qualities—thus it still has Essence or Form. What are those qualities? The qualities of marble. The Essence or Form of what remains is marble-ness. Now, suppose we could remove this Essence too. Suppose we could take the marble-ness away from this piece of stone. What should we have? Pure stone—not marble or granite or limestone, but pure stone, the substance underlying all stone. Of course, we can never see pure stone on earth. All manifest stone has to be some particular *form* of stone—marble or jade or flint. But is this Stone, even stripped of the Essence of any particular stone, pure substance? It is not, because it still has *qualities*—the qualities of stone-ness.

Now, in theory, we could go on stripping away qualities or Forms

---

truly substantialist in the way that that of the more idealistic Tennyson was. The question here is not one of personal belief or inclination, but of the underlying world-view inculcated by the surrounding culture.

or Essences, until we were left with pure substance, or *matter*—
Materia Prima as the Scholastics called it. What would this pure
matter be like? Clearly it would not be like *anything*. It would have
no Form, no Essence, no *qualities*. So, it would have no color, no
weight, no texture, no sound, no scent. It would not be hard or
soft, cool or hot, rough or smooth. Obviously, then, we could not
see it, feel it, smell it, taste it, or hear it. We could not perceive it in
any way. Indeed, it is not a *physical* thing at all.

All physical things must have Essence *and* substance.[2] The very
definition of a manifest thing is that it is a combination of Essence
and substance, a Form impressed on matter. Pure Essence and pure
substance of necessity lie outside manifestation—which is not the
same thing as saying that they do not exist.

---

2. It is interesting to note, in this context, the findings of scientists who have attempted to probe the inner nature of matter. The more we learn about subatomic
particles, the more they seem to defy all normal physical description. They seem at
times to behave like particles and at other times to behave like waves. They do
things that would normally be called physical impossibilities, and at times the
very laws of cause and effect appear to be inverted, with an event that is caused
happening *before* the event that causes it. Scientists are compelled to surmise that
these are not physical entities at all in any sense of the term that means anything to
us. What they seem to be, we are told, is "pieces of pure information".

Now this is patently absurd. How can information exist on its own with nothing
to inform?—and remember, there *is* nothing for these subatomic particles to inform,
because they are supposed to constitute *everything* that is. According to the only view
acceptable to a purely material science, every existing thing must be built up from
them and nothing else. Scientists themselves admit the logical impossibility of the
thing—the fact that the whole mechanistic, materialistic system of modern science
turns out to be based upon an absurdity. The very laws of cause and effect upon
which science is based fall to pieces as we reach the foundations of matter itself.

Nevertheless, this description makes perfect sense in the light of primordial
science. Essence *is* precisely pure information. It informs—forms from within—
every material entity. Essence is Form—or information—working on substance,
and substance can only be seen when the light of Essence is shining on it: we can
only perceive marble, for example, because of its qualities—its hardness, color,
weight, stone-ness.

At the subatomic level we cannot detect the substance upon which Essence is
working. This is because there is some truth in the scientist's belief that he is "getting to the very building blocks of matter itself", and while he is not, and could
not be, at the level of pure substance or *Prima Materia,* he is seeing matter stripped

Now what is true of every individual entity is equally true of the manifest cosmos as a whole. The Poles of Essence and substance, which may be called the upper and lower poles of being, both lie outside the domain of manifest existence; yet both are necessary to manifest existence—are, indeed, the sole causes and determinants of manifest existence.

Yet while the manifest cosmos cannot possibly exist at either the Pole of pure Essence or the Pole of pure substance, it can certainly be *closer* to one Pole or to the other. And the process of manifestation consists precisely of a movement from proximity to the Pole of Essence toward proximity to the Pole of substance.

This means that the movement of time is always from the subtle to the gross, from the inward to the outward, from the spiritual to the material. This, when we consider it, is exactly what manifestation necessarily means. Manifestation is precisely the bringing into outward or material existence of those things that were originally contained *in principio* within the Absolute.

Any given cycle of the history of humanity (or of any equivalent being) will necessarily reflect the great cycle of manifestation itself. Thus it will begin in close proximity to the Pole of Essence, being

---

of many of its Essential qualities. Consequently, at this level, matter is no longer prehensible, and all that can be seen is the low-level action of Essence, which appears to be acting on its own as 'pure information', but is in fact in-forming matter at a very rudimentary level.

There is an irony—but in fact it is something more than a mere accidental irony—in the fact that modern science, which bases itself exclusively upon a purely material and quantitative approach and upon the assumption that everything can be explained from the side of matter, ignoring Essence altogether, should, upon approaching what ought to be, as it were, its own domain *par excellence*—the nearest we can get in manifestation to 'pure matter'—run headlong into the problem of Essence and see its material and quantitative axioms go up in smoke.

It is also important for us to realize from the outset that when we speak of Essence and substance as the fundamental principles of cosmic manifestation, we are not talking merely of philosophical abstractions or ancient notions that have been superseded by modern science; we are speaking of vital truths which have always been true, and which, while they may have *seemed* to be rendered obsolete in the comfortable, closed world of eighteenth- and nineteenth-century mechanistic materialism, the findings of twentieth-century atomic and astrophysics reveal to be absolutely necessary to an adequate and coherent explanation of being.

oriented to spiritual existence, and will gradually descend into ever more material forms of existence. This is exemplified in the doctrine of the Four Ages, which describes the descent from the Golden Age (gold being the metal of the Sun, and thus of the Spirit) to the Iron Age (iron being the metal belonging to Mars and the masculine principle). It is interesting to note that this symbolism—like many other indications of the original feminine perspective—remains unchanged in patriarchal traditions.

Nor should we imagine that the increasing 'solidification' inherent in our historical cycle is merely a question of an increasing materialism or lack of spirituality on the part of human beings. What takes place is necessarily a genuine hardening or consolidation of the terrestrial environment itself; so that humanity is living under very different earthly conditions now from those that prevailed even in the Bronze Age. It is for this reason that many aspects of the accounts of earlier times are dismissed by modern writers as 'mythical'. Many ancient narratives are, of course, mythical in the true sense and were written with purposes very far removed from those of mundane history, but numerous statements of fact—such as the great longevity of early figures (usually changed from female to male in patriarchal accounts), often running into hundreds of years, the prevalence and great effectiveness of sorcery, or, as noted earlier, the existence of creatures that, being of a subtler order than the creatures of the present era, have left no trace perceptible to modern senses—are to be taken entirely at face value and must be attributed to the changed conditions brought about by the consolidation of the terrestrial environment.

One of the traditional symbols of cosmic manifestation is the pyramid. Pyramidal structures were built in places other than Egypt—for example in ancient America—often in stepped form, representing the degrees of existence ranged between the point and the base.

The pyramid is a figure of the cosmos itself, as seen both from a spatial and a temporal perspective. The top represents that part of the cosmos which is nearest to Pure Essence—the single, unified Point that contains within itself the whole structure (note that however small a section may be cut from the top of a pyramid by a horizontal stroke, it will be an image of the entire pyramid in miniature). The base represents that part of manifestation which is as near as possible to pure substance. It is square—the square being the geometrical figure representing matter—and covers the widest area of any part of the pyramid, representing the quantitative expansion of manifestation.

The point of the pyramid represents a maximum of Essence or quality and a minimum of substance or quantity, while the base represents a maximum of quantity and a minimum of quality. Each consecutive stage between these two (whether the pyramid be tiered or not) represents some level between these two.

We may note that 'level' here may mean one of two things. If the spatial symbolism of cosmic hierarchy be envisaged, then it will mean macrocosmically a 'plane of being' or degree of existence, and microcosmically, within the human domain, a level of social being between the sacred priestess-queen at the apex and the humblest and most numerous section of the population at the base. The pyramid thus will also represent the social hierarchy, and the passage of celestial influence and divine love from each level to the level immediately below it in the Golden Chain of the sacred feminine social order. At the same time, from the point of view of the spiritual quest, the Ascent of the Pyramid will represent the progress of the soul from the material level of the base, through successive stages to the Realization of the apex.

On the other hand, if a temporal perspective be envisaged, the descent of the pyramid (according to the natural law of gravity) will represent macrocosmically the continual expansion and consolidation of cosmic manifestation and microcosmically, within the human sphere, the inevitable movement of the historical cycle from the qualitative civilization of the earliest times to the quantitative order of the last days. The 'levels' of the pyramid in this case will therefore be successive eras or stages in the process of manifestation.

It will be readily noted that the Pyramid, like all traditional symbols, represents many different things, all of which are simply applications, within different domains of manifestation, of precisely the same Reality. We shall also see shortly that, while the late-patriarchal world is entirely ignorant of the traditional science of symbolism, its own doctrines and practices also reflect, in many different ways, the Inversion of the Pyramid: this is inevitable, for the modern world can do nothing other than reflect eternal Reality, albeit in inverted or perverted form.

It may be of interest to add at this point that if accounts of the remarkable preservative and fecundating properties of the pyramidal form are correct (and we have no cause to doubt them), this would be entirely in keeping with the symbolism of the pyramid as a figure of the Golden Order of the universe—the very cosmic-hierarchical structure that maintains all things in being. And if the pyramid has retained its symbolic-ritual effectiveness on the material plane at a time when that of many other figures has become greatly diminished owing to the extreme 'consolidation' of the late Iron Age, this is undoubtedly due to the fact that the 'static' and 'conservative' nature of the pyramid has served at once to preserve its own ritual effectiveness and to render it more 'adaptable' to a consolidated age.[3]

Quite obviously, the point of the pyramid is single, while the base contains an indefinite multiplicity of such points. The apex is, in fact, that point in the manifest cosmos (or in history, or in whatever

---

3. For the pyramid is by no means the only traditional symbol we might have used to illustrate the principles being discussed here. The more 'dynamic' symbol of the wheel would serve, in a slightly different aspect, precisely the same purpose. In this case, all that is said of the apex of the pyramid may be applied to the central point of the wheel, and of the base of the pyramid to the wheel's outer rim. Here ('spatially'), each spoke of the wheel represents an entity, each having its origin in the Archetypal realm (the hub) and passing through every level of existence (for geometrically we may depict any number of concentric circles between the rim and the hub) until it is manifest on the material plane (the rim). The unmoving axle-point at the center of the wheel is where our entire universal system has its point of connexion with yet superior realms, and the axle itself is the World Axis, linking one world (wheel) to another. The relation to the symbolism of the Cross (see note, p.40) is obvious, especially when we realize that the cross itself may also be seen in horizontal mode, in which case its center is the point at which a third, vertical, beam transfixes it. We mention this primarily that the reader may begin to understand that traditional symbolism is a vast, interlocking language, by no means arbitrary, but as precise as a calculus; and that every traditional artefact, such as a wheel, is not merely a utilitarian object, but an intelligible expression, a contemplative 'support', and an effective element in the 'magical' ritual which comprises the whole of the life of a Traditional Society.

else may be in question) at which multiplicity is least and essential qualities are greatest, while the base is that area where multiplicity is as great as possible, and essential qualities are least. In other words, the base contains the greatest possible number of entities, each as little differentiated as possible and containing a minimum of qualities. In the universal order, the summit governs the base in two senses. From the static or hierarchical perspective, the summit is the ruler of the base, and from the temporal or developmental perspective, the summit is the *cause* of the base. In other words, the summit comes first, and then produces the level of the pyramid immediately below it; then each successively lower level is produced from the level above, until finally the base is the ultimate product of the summit.

Traditionally, the concept *first* always bears these two senses— first in point of time or of logic and first in the sense of ruling and governing. So the Greek *arche* means both 'first' or 'early' (as in *arch*aeology, the study of the first or earliest times) and 'ruler' (as in mon*archy,* hier*archy,* matri*archy,* and so on). Similarly, *princess* comes from *primus,* meaning 'first', as does *prime* minister (the *first,* i.e., ruling, minister), and so forth. An *Arche*type is both the *original* of an earthly entity and its *ruling principle.*

In the symbolism of the pyramid, the apex is the *arche,* the First Point in the two senses of 'original' and 'ruling'.

As we should expect, the late-patriarchal ideology inverts the Golden Order, attempting to stand the pyramid on its head. In all things, it attempts to make the base of the pyramid the *arche,* being either the *cause* or the *ruler* of the apex. In the most fundamental sense, it does this by declaring substance, or matter, to be the original principle, and holding that all forms, all intelligence, all organization, have 'evolved' blindly out of brute matter.

Beginning from this fundamental inversion, it is inevitable that whatever aspect of being is considered, the late-patriarchal world will apply to it the fundamental symbol of the inverted pyramid.

Thus, in physics, it declares the smallest subatomic particles (those elements, in other words, that are necessarily most numerous and most lacking in differentiating qualities) to be the very foundation-stones of the universe itself (the *arche).* Logically it believes that if we want to know why things are what they are, we must first observe these particles and then work upwards. The traditional view is, of course, the precise reverse of this. While not having the least desire to deny the *existence* of subatomic particles, it is evident that the forms they take on, progressively more elaborate and sophisticated at each higher level of microscopic existence, are not inherent in the particles themselves, or in their random combination, but come from the opposite Pole of existence, from the Essence that gives form to all things. To imagine 'the key to existence' may be found in subatomic particles is like imagining that the grand strategy of an army may be discovered by talking to private soldiers. The grand strategy, of course, emanates from the other end of the hierarchy—from the generals and ultimately from the Princess herself.

Similarly in biology, the late-patriarchal view wishes to find the *arche,* or origin, of all the elaborated and highly sophisticated forms of biological life, from the most complex flower to the dazzling complexity of the higher animals, in those life forms that are most numerous and least differentiated—the single-celled creatures.

Again, in the sphere of politics, late-patriarchal 'democracy' pretends (and it can never be more than a pretense) to make the *arche,* the ultimate ruling principle, out of the 'common masses'— the most numerous and least qualitatively differentiated section of the commonweal.[4]

---

4. We are certainly not saying that 'democracy' is simply an ill, any more than we are saying that patriarchy itself is simply an ill. Some degree of 'democratic' culture—in the sense of an increasing cultural orientation toward the mass of the people—is both inevitable at the end of the age, and may be productive of many incidental benefits, just as the Normal or non-traditional society was productive of such cultural benefits as the nineteenth-century literary and artistic tradition. The popular arts of the twentieth century, which are probably its greatest contribution to the fruition of the historical cycle, are closely bound up with its 'democratic' character, and we have every respect for these things on their own level (see Chapter Eight, *passim*).

However, this is only nominally connected with the political fantasy of 'the rule of the people', which on the 'exterior' level is nothing more than the 'cover story' for the real (financial and highly undemocratic) operations of power, but like all twentieth-century fables has its roots deep in the metaphysical inversions of substantialism.

Whichever way we turn, we shall see that the underlying theories of the late-patriarchal world are founded on the inversion of the pyramid, on a seizing upon the most multiple and least qualitatively differentiated order of being in any given sphere, and attempting to make it into the *arche*. And in each case, this inversion is merely a consequence or application of the fundamental fallacy of believing form to be a mere derivative of matter.

*

Plato, following tradition, taught that there are two worlds: the *sensible* world and the *Intelligible* world. The sensible world is the world we live in, made up of objects perceived by our five *senses*. The Intelligible world, being non-material, cannot be perceived by our senses, but only by our highest faculty, which is pure Intelligence.[5]

The sensible world contains the things we see and hear and

---

5. It is important to understand that there is a radical difference between the Traditional and the 'modernist' definitions of 'intelligence'. According to the modern doctrine, all *information* comes to us through the five senses, in the form of *sense-data*. The function of the intelligence is limited to 'processing' that data. According to the traditional view what modern people call 'intelligence' is only the lower mental faculty or reason (*ratio* the measurer). True Intelligence is prehensive. It *perceives* truths unavailable to the senses. It is through the Intelligence, for example, that we 'see' the Archetypes. Intelligence, indeed, is our highest perceptive faculty and is that part of us which is continuous with the Divine. It is the Solar faculty, which is why Intellect is associated traditionally with the heart. Reason (lunar) is situated in the head. Pure Truth is innate in us, which is why Plato, in common with all tradition, teaches that "all learning is remembering". The Greek for Truth is *alethea*: unforgetting, *lethe* being forgetfulness. The Tibetan lama, teaching a truth, makes the sign of the thunderbolt destroying ignorance, for the Truth is already in us; only the veil of ignorance keeps us from it. Such is the very meaning of *intel-lect:* "reading within".

Necessarily the substantialist must deny the Intelligence. Descartes proposes a complete skepticism in which we doubt all things. From there he says that one thing at least we can know: *cogito ergo sum,* "I think, therefore I am". However, there are no logical steps beyond this. In order to reinstate the normal thought-processes, Descartes has to abandon pure skepticism and re-import some of the intuitive axioms of thought. For our very confidence in reason and the senses is itself a primary Intellectual intuition which cannot itself be derived from either reason or the senses. Without this, thought—even substantialist thought—is impossible. The substantialist attempt to deny the Intelligence does not stand up to rigorous examination.

touch, while the Intelligible world contains the Forms of which those material things are but the shadows. Material objects derive their shape and all their qualities precisely from their Archetypes *(eidei)*—the Forms of the Intelligible world. Every thing that exists is the material reflection of an Archetype—or rather a portion of matter in-formed by an Archetype.

It is clear from this that the Intelligible world, in relation to our material domain, represents the Pole of Essence—or that it is another way of expressing the same thing. When we speak of the Pole of Essence, we are regarding Essence as a single principle as compared to substance. When we speak of the Intelligible world, or the realm of the Archetypes, we are regarding the pure Light of Essence, or Form, as it is refracted into manifestation: that is, as the variety of distinct Forms that make up a universe.

These two perspectives are complementary, and both are necessary for a full understanding of the principles involved. The sensible world, in which we live, is the world of flux and change, dominated by time. The Intelligible world is beyond time: perfect, changeless, and eternal. The Archetypes reflected upon our plane of being are not seen as they really are, but are always clouded and distorted, like an image reflected in an imperfect medium. Thus, when we see the sun reflected in a lake, it may be misshapen and distorted. That is not because the true sun in the sky is misshapen or distorted, but because the medium in which it is reflected is not still. The Eternal Forms are constant and perfect, but their reflections upon the earthly plane are constantly shimmering and distorting in the flux and change of matter.

At times the reflection of a form may change so much that it is scarcely recognizable as the original Archetype—this may happen particularly in the sphere of human artefacts and human social functions during non-traditional periods—nevertheless, every form in the universe *is* a reflection, whether relatively pure or relatively distorted, of an eternal Form. For it is from these Forms, from the Intelligible world, from the Pole of Essence, that all form derives. Therein lies the very Principle of Form, and without it the universe would be, as the Bible expresses it, "without form and void".

Every thing, be it an animal, a house, a flower, a star, a crown, a bridge, a tree, or a lion, is the reflection of an Archetype, or else it could not be. It would simply remain un-formed matter, which, as we have seen, can have no physical existence.

And we may note that there are two distinct forms of Archetypal reflection mentioned in the above list—those occurring 'naturally' and those created by human hands. In each case the principle is the same, for it matters not whether the Forms are reflected directly upon the earth, like trees and flowers and mountains, or whether they are embodied through the agency of the human Intellect, which is the surrogate of the Divine.

There are yet other ways in which maid can mediate in the manifestation of the Archetypes on earth. The stories she tells contain Archetypal motifs and events; and in her own person she may embody such Archetypes as the Mother, the Princess, the Servant, the Child, the Maker, the Lover, the Priestess, and all the fundamental human Forms.

At this stage it is important to warn against a confusion that the substantialist outlook makes almost inevitable, and that has been put into particularly beguiling and specious form by the work of the late Dr. C. G. Jung.

When considering Archetypes mediated through maid, whether embodied by her directly or contained in her stories or the work of her hands, it is vital to remember that these Archetypes are *not* the products of the human mind—whether of individual minds or of a 'collective unconscious'. These Archetypes are no more *products* of the human mind than are the Archetypes of an eagle, a blade of grass, or the moon. The human Intellect *perceives* these Archetypes, just as the human eye perceives the moon. Their images exist in the human mind just as the image of the moon does, but they did not originate there, any more than the moon did.

All forms, whether manifested in gross matter or in the human psyche, originate at the Pole of Essence. There is, and can be, no other source for Form. All forms are eternal. The Princess predates this present humanity just as the eagle and the dove predate this present earth.

Chapter Six

THE MYTH OF THE MODERN WORLD

EVERY CIVILIZATION lives by myths. A myth may be defined as a picture-story that encapsulates the fundamental beliefs of a people. But myths are of two kinds. The first kind is the genuine myth. This kind of story is told because certain truths can only be conveyed in the form of myth. Certain truths transcend the merely rational level and can be grasped only by pure Intellect, or else in the form of stories that bring the everyday, rational-emotional soul as close to transcendent Truth as she is able to come.

These myths are, either directly or ultimately, divine revelations. They include such things as the various Creation Stories of the different traditions. It is an error (but not usually a very serious one) to take them too literally,[1] but it is a far greater error to imagine that they are simply untrue, in the way that a false statement about history would be untrue. The entire *raison d'être* of authentic myth is that it is *more* true than mere contingent history. We may say that

---

1. In the case of Fundamentalist Christianity, the error is a little more serious than is normally the position, precisely because this view was adopted in reaction to the substantialist criticism of the Bible (notably the oddly named 'Higher Criticism' of the late-nineteenth-century German Liberal Protestant school whose precepts came to dominate twentieth-century 'theology') which criticizes and in many cases denies the historicity of Scriptural narratives. Unfortunately the reaction was made on precisely the same substantialist level as the criticisms themselves, claiming that the Bible is entirely accurate in point of mundane historical fact and is to be taken wholly literally, consequently denying symbolic, mystical, and other traditional levels of interpretation and thus immeasurably impoverishing the rich and many-layered appeal of traditional Scriptures to the human soul. Nonetheless, a naïve belief in the literal accuracy of Genesis is far healthier for the psyche than the spiritually empty hotchpotch of half-digested paperback scientism believed by most modern people.

It is worthy of note that both the 'Higher Criticism' and the Fundamentalism produced in reaction to it were direct results of the new substantialist mentality of the later nineteenth century, brought about by the seismic change that followed the introduction of the pseudomythos discussed in this chapter. This is significant particularly because it demonstrates how even the Fundamentalists who explicitly rejected the pseudomythos were nonetheless formed by the atmosphere it created.

history tells of events that might or might not have happened, whereas myths tell of 'events' (or rather, transcendent Realities couched in the form of events) that cannot *not* be.

The second kind of myth, which can come into being only in an untraditional society, is the false myth or pseudomythos. This form of myth has no connexion with transcendent reality. It conveys no ultimate truth. It merely conveys in story-picture form the ideology of a society that has lost its vital connexion with its metaphysical taproot. Such story-pictures are needed precisely because myths are a fundamental requirement of the human psyche, which is made for Truth, and therefore for Myth.

The pseudomythos may be true or false on its own level: that is, as history or biology or whatever it purports to be; but it is manifestly false at the level at which it is *really* operating in the psyche: that is, as an artificial substitute for authentic Myth, an explanation of the nature and pattern of being. Of such false myths may it truly be said: "I asked for bread and you gave me a stone", for instead of nourishing the soul with Truth as real Myths do, they freeze and petrify it with falsehood or with trivia.

The fundamental pseudomythos of the twentieth century is the Story of Evolution. C. S. Lewis, in an essay entitled "The Funeral of a Great Myth", has demonstrated how the progress/evolution story, as retailed in schools and by the mass media and accepted as one of the few incontestable truths of the supposedly 'questioning' modern world, exhibits all the fundamental characteristics of the classic hero-myth.

From the philosophical point of view, the salient characteristic of modern evolutionism (for there are, as we shall see, other and truer interpretations of the term 'evolution') is that it puts forward an account of being (on the biological plane) that derives Form entirely from matter and annihilates the Essential dimension of being.

It is precisely because of this that evolutionism met with such spectacular success on its first introduction to the Western world. Unconsciously, and in some cases consciously, the West had been looking for a substantialist *mythos,* which would bring the mythic (or story-picture) dimension of its thinking into line with the increasingly substantialist philosophy that had dominated it since the seventeenth century.

Several attempts were made, long before Charles Darwin, to concoct some sort of substantialist *mythos* along broadly 'evolutionist' lines. One of the most complete of these attempts was made by Charles Darwin's grandfather, Erasmus Darwin, who constructed the theory of evolution, not so much from solid evidence as from the philosophical precepts of substantialism. The idea that Charles Darwin was compelled to his evolutionist conclusions by the evidence he discovered is quite unfounded. He set out on the *Beagle* with his grandfather's substantialist *mythos* firmly implanted in his mind, seeking the 'evidence' to confirm it.

Once this 'evidence' was presented, it was hailed by a generation of substantialists as the answer to their prayers. Its success had the emotional weight of two centuries of substantialism behind it, and was as easy to resist as an avalanche. In vain, a minority of scientists pointed out the numerous flaws and contradictions in the theory and appealed for a more rigorously scientific approach to the subject. They were attacking not a piece of science, but the new 'religion' of the West.

Yet the passing years and the various researches undertaken to fill in the gaps in Darwin's work have done little to confirm the theory. On the contrary, Paul Lemoine, editor of Volume V (on 'Living Organisms') of the *Encyclopédie Française,* summed up the modern evidence thus: "This exposition shows that the theory of evolution is impossible. In reality, despite appearances, no one any longer believes in it... Evolution is a sort of dogma whose priests no longer believe in it, though they uphold it for the sake of their flocks."

This is not to postulate a 'conspiracy' among biologists, but simply to say that the terminology of evolution has become a convention: "One speaks, without attaching any importance to it, of evolution to denote linkage—of more evolved, less evolved in the sense of more perfect, less perfect, because it is the conventional language".[2] The convention is easily accepted, since scientists are as conditioned by the modern myth as anyone else. But a real belief in evolution is difficult if one is in possession of the actual facts.

Evolution divides into two classes: micro-evolution and mega-evolution. The former concerns relatively small-scale changes within

---

2. Lemoine, *ibid.*

a species (such as the celebrated case of the butterflies that changed from white to dark brown when their environment became dirtied by industrial effluents, so often quoted by evolutionists as a triumphant 'proof' of their theory). Nobody contests the occurrence of this simple adaptation. Mega-evolution postulates greater transformations from one major class of animal to another—it is this second form of evolution upon which the modern myth rests. No known instance of mega-evolution has ever been shown to have taken place, and, indeed, the observation of micro-evolution indicates that there are definite limits in nature to the extent of possible transformation, and that, having run their course, transformations inevitably reach a dead end. As one commentator put it: "Mega-evolution is really a philosophy dating from the days of biological ignorance." All the so-called 'proofs of evolution' are based on micro-evolution.

To take another aspect of the question, the fossil record flatly contradicts evolutionist notions. One unequivocal feature is the abruptness with which new classes of animals make their appearance. There is no evidence of gradual change from one species to another. Some evolutionists have accounted for this by putting forward theories of 'explosive evolution'—suggesting that nature herself has the power suddenly to throw up a new species. This is compatible with the theory discussed on page 83, and similarly invalidates evolutionism as a substantialist pseudomythos.

Of course, when we turn from the serious scientist to the popular evolutionism promulgated by the schools and the mass media, and unquestioningly believed by the mass of the populace, the errors and deceptions multiply. The old charts of "the evolution of the horse", long since discredited among serious scientists, are still put forward as uncontested fact; and we find everywhere the notorious 'reconstructions' of the brutish face of Neanderthal Man, of which the American palaeontologist Professor A. E. Hooton has said: "You can with equal facility model on a Neanderthaloid skull the features of a chimpanzee or the lineaments of a philosopher. These alleged reconstructions of ancient types of man have little, if any, scientific value, and are likely only to mislead the public."

As Jean Piveteau, Professor of Palaeontology at the Sorbonne, put it: "[The science of facts] cannot accept any of the different theories which seek to explain evolution. It even finds itself in opposition to each one of these theories. There is something here which is both disappointing and disquieting."

But if the evidence for evolution in general is unscientific, the evidence for the evolution of humanity is virtually non-existent; yet it continues to be taught as 'established fact' to adults and children alike. One children's encyclopaedia tells us: "Early man probably lived in the bare open, hiding behind rocks and in caves, and this is perhaps the reason why we do not find his fossilized remains mixed up with the remains of the animals which inhabited the same world. Whatever the reason, all that we know of man for hundreds of thousands of years is derived from a few very primitive flint instruments and from fragments of bones and skulls which may not be the bones of our ancestors at all, but the remains of apes."

Nonetheless, the encyclopaedia continues to treat speculations based on this minuscule evidence as established reality, and prints imaginative artistic depictions of 'early man', and charts of the 'evolutionary process' to fix the concept firmly in the young mind.

What is never mentioned is the huge body of evidence that clearly points to the existence of people of modern type long before Homo Sapiens is supposed to have evolved (see Cremo and Thompson's *Forbidden Archeology*). Nowhere, except perhaps in a book of 'curious facts', does the child have the opportunity to read of the imprints of shoes, showing traces of strong thread, in two separate coal seams in the Gobi Desert and in Nevada, each estimated to be about *fifteen million* years old—when the crudest 'ape-men' are not supposed to have evolved until two million years ago. Neither does she learn of the various artefacts—nails, gold wire, even a perfectly ground optical lens—found in various parts of the world in geological strata of immense antiquity. Remember that the theory of 'early man' is based on a tiny handful of evidence, much of which is ambiguous. Yet another handful of quite unambiguous evidence is dismissed as 'unexplainable curiosities' because it does not fit in with the modern myth. What other science selects its evidence in this way?

Far more important than the material evidence is the fact that evolution is a metaphysical impossibility. That is to say, it contradicts the inner laws of being that govern the manifestation of the material universe itself (though this is not true of those modern forms of evolutionism which hold that forms were inherent in genetic structures from the beginning). Material science, of course, knows nothing of this point, but it may well be asked why the modern world persists in clinging to "a philosophy dating from the days of biological ignorance". In physics, chemistry, and all other modern sciences, Victorian notions were revolutionized in the twentieth century. In each case it has been admitted that the universe is infinitely subtler and more mysterious than the old mechanistic theories supposed. But evolutionism, despite all evidence, has been preserved virtually unchanged as "a sort of dogma".

Why is this so? Precisely, of course, because it *is* a dogma, clung to with the same tenacity with which Fundamentalists cling to an absurdly literal interpretation of the Book of Genesis. Nor is the case helped by the fact that, for the modern mind, these two forms of literalism appear to be the only possibilities open to them. As Professor D. M. S. Watson, put it, evolution "is accepted by most biologists not because it has been observed to occur or... can be proved by logically coherent evidence to be true, but because the only alternative, specific creation, is clearly incredible."[3]

What is "incredible" in such a case is, of course, largely a question of emotional predispositions and of what ideas one has heard repeated and assumed by every 'authoritative' source until they appear natural. If one lays aside the years of evolutionist conditioning for a moment and looks at the question with a fresh, questioning mind, surely the idea that the intricacy of human intelligence should be derived from an entirely *unintelligent* process of blind 'natural selection' is one of the more incredible things human beings have ever been asked to believe. Again, when one observes

---

3. Some scientists, indeed, go much further. The famous biologist Jean Rostand writes: "I firmly believe—because I see no means of doing otherwise—that mammals came from lizards, and lizards from fish; but when I declare and when I think such a thing I try not to avoid seeing its indigestible enormity and I prefer to leave vague the origin of these scandalous metamorphoses rather than add to their improbability with that of a ludicrous explanation."

any of the countless million productions of nature, even one of the simplest such as a sycamore 'key' spinning like a helicopter through the air: are we really supposed to believe—intuitively—that such a wonderful piece of aerodynamic design happened by the accident of natural selection—when we know perfectly well that hundreds of other species of tree survive perfectly well with no such device or any equivalent? Again, is it *intuitively* likely that the enormous fecundity, beauty and minute construction of thousands upon thousands of highly differentiated flower species is nothing more than a blindly evolved device for "attracting insects to ensure pollination", especially when we know that bees and other insects will visit small plants with no flower just as readily as large ones with bright and elaborate flowers, even when the two are side by side, and that all pollen-gathering insects will desert the most brilliant displays of flowers for a dump of waste industrial sugar?

If simple credibility is a criterion, does it not seem incredible to explain away the fecundity, the artistry, the sheer *intelligence* of the cosmic creative principle with a utilitarian hypothesis that reduces all form to function and fails to take account of its *needless* diversity and magnificence? Does not such a hypothesis seem to be an example of masculine-materialist banality and monomania extended to the point of absurdity?

*

The scientific objections to evolutionism are not of the first importance. The fundamental objection is that evolutionism is contrary to the laws of metaphysics: and if material science contradicts metaphysics, material science must inevitably be wrong (except where, as in the case of Copernican astronomy, there is a confusion of levels and the contradiction is only apparent). Scientific 'truths' were never intended to be more than working hypotheses, which may be overturned at any time by new discoveries, and often are. Science, at best, deals in relative or conjectural truth. Metaphysics deals in the fundamental laws of being and in truths that could not be otherwise; its basis is not the finite and fallible senses and the conjectures of merely human reason, but the direct perception of pure Intellect, which is continuous between the human and the Divine. Its guarantee is that, in all its essentials, and allowing for differences of spiritual 'language', it is the same in all traditional cultures the world over, even those that have had no historical contact with the others (such as the 'shamanism' of the Australian Aboriginals or the traditions of the pre-Columbian Americas). Therefore, even if evolutionism were apparently fully demonstrated by science (which, as we have seen, is very far from being the case), metaphysical law would still take precedence as being *necessarily* true rather than merely rendered temporarily probable by the current balance of evidence.[4]

When evolutionism was first introduced many scientists were half-consciously aware of the metaphysical violation involved. They resisted it, not on religious grounds, but because they had a strong intuition that a species had about it something absolute, that infinite mutation was a violation of some fundamental natural law. This, in fact, was the most difficult hurdle that the fledgling pseudomythos had to overcome.

These objections *were* quickly overcome because they were not founded in Intellectual principle. Rather, they were vestiges of the Essentialist view of life that was still surprisingly strong in the middle of the nineteenth century, but had crumbled almost completely by the end of it.

The reason for the persistence of the Essentialist outlook was precisely the lack of a substantialist pseudomythos. While most abstract thinking was broadly substantialist, the 'myths', the story-pictures, upon which the psyche was fed were still fundamentally Essentialist.

Before the introduction of the new pseudomythos, the human psyche, however much it might adhere to an outward substantialism, was still inwardly confronted with the problem of Form. Where does Form itself come from? The question was rarely specifically asked, but the underlying knowledge that in the Forms of all the things about us lay something beyond the substantial world, a trace of the Divine, was never wholly lost. The Romantic Movement, for example, would have been meaningless without it.

Evolutionism demolished the question of Form, by abusively

---

4. This is precisely what Aristotle meant when he wrote in *Posterior Analytics:* "The Intellect is truer than science."

deriving the greater from the less. It situated Form itself wholly on the level of substance, claiming it to be nothing more than a product of the flux and change of matter. It eliminated the vertical dimension from the universe, explaining everything in terms of the horizontal flow of time and matter.

Nonetheless, there is a curious irony in the fact that even this anti-Essentialist pseudomythos owed a good deal of its force to surreptitious and illegitimate borrowings from the Essentialist outlook. Evolution took, in the minds of most people, the form of a pseudo-teleology: a purposeful force headed in a generally 'upward' and beneficial direction; a strange, demythologized parody of an intelligent directing force; an atheistic half-God.

Such a view is, of course, illogical and illegitimate, and it is against this sort of thinking that Nietzsche is protesting in the passage with which we opened this book—protesting, of course, from the side of pure substantialism against the pseudo-Essentialist adulteration of the doctrine.

Nevertheless, as we have said, few people could, or can, bear the bleakness of the pure substantialist vision presented so accurately by Nietzsche, and in most modern minds resides a warm, foggy muddle in which all the fundamentals of substantialism are present but sweetened slightly by soft, squashy bits of fake Essentialism. For the human psyche is made for Essentialism, and she cannot easily survive without it.

The very choice of the word 'evolution' is pseudo-Essentialist. 'E-volution' means literally an 'unrolling' or 'unfolding'—a very strange word considering what the theory is really supposed to mean. We might reasonably speak, say, of the 'evolution' of an oak tree from an acorn: in other words the unfolding or realization of the potentialities that were present in the acorn from the start.

Evolution in this sense is a perfectly legitimate part of traditional teaching. Everything evolves—a chicken from an egg; a flower from a seed; a civilization from an initial supernatural revelation that founds the principles on which it is to be based. The Historical Cycle and indeed cosmic manifestation itself are examples of evolution.

We would, of course, contest the modern idea that evolution proceeds from the less to the greater. A civilization is greatest at its beginnings: the time of its Prophet or *Avatar,* when the divine lightning strikes the world. Islam was greatest in the first days, when the Prophet walked the earth, and Christianity was greatest in the time of Jesus and the Apostles. Both revelations gave rise to mighty civilizations—the caliphates of Baghdad and Cordova; the great cities, universities, and cathedrals of the Middle Ages—but those were developments of the outward and material potentialities of the civilizations concerned, a thing that happens when the first spiritual impetus is lost.

Similarly with the Historical Cycle: the Iron Age develops the most outward and material potentialities of the cycle, ending with modern technics and world-industrialism; but these outward developments take place only at the expense of much higher and more valuable things.

Nonetheless, we may put down this disagreement with the modern 'evolutionist' to a difference of perspective rather than a dispute about fact. The late-patriarchal mind values outward material development above spiritual purity and the vertical dimension of being. While no true Muslim would see the great days of Baghdad as superior to the time of the Prophet in the desert, the modernist certainly would.

On the fact of evolution as a continual *outward* and horizontal development—a continual *growth* in purely quantitative terms—of the potentialities inherent in anything from a flower to a civilization to the whole of cosmic manifestation itself, the Essentialist cannot but agree. As mentioned, the word 'evolution' means unrolling or unfolding, and therefore implies that whatever is unfolded must have been there *in principio* from the beginning. But that is precisely what Darwinian evolution is *not* supposed to mean. Darwinian evolution is supposed to mean the genuine (and metaphysically impossible) derivation of the greater from the less—the creation of the entire living world by itself, out of itself, from nothing, or practically nothing.

If it does not mean that, then it is not a substantialist pseudomythos, and if it does mean that, why call it 'evolution', which means the opposite?

We are not merely quibbling over a word. The use of the term 'evolution' is highly significant and characterizes the entire nature of the pseudomythos. It *is* a substantialist pseudomythos, but it has always been sugared with just enough pseudo-teleology to make it palatable to the Essentialist soul of maid. Words are more magical than we think, and although not one person in a hundred is aware of the derivation of 'evolution', the choice of word nonetheless subconsciously conveys its pseudo-Essentialist message, and, we have no doubt, conforms to a psychic 'movement' far deeper than anything Darwin (grandfather or grandson) can have had in mind.[5]

Curiously, there are signs that 'evolutionism' may be moving closer to the true sense of the term, as some modern evolutionists, seeking ways of resolving the ever-widening flaws in the theory, have postulated that all the genetic information for the innumerable species, with their countless attributes, was in fact contained within the DNA of the first single-celled creatures.[6] This overcomes

---

5. On the choice of words of the profoundest metaphysical (or, which is the same thing in reverse, 'diabolical') significance by scientists who can have had no conscious idea of what they were doing, it is fascinating to consider the naming of the 'outer' planets Pluto, Neptune, and Uranus and—by quite different scientists—the corresponding metallic elements, plutonium, neptunium, and uranium. Not only does this answer generally to the traditional correspondence of planets to metals (Sun-gold, Moon-silver, Venus-copper, Mars-iron, etc.), but it has a much fuller and more sinister significance. The outer planets lie beyond Saturn, the furthest of the traditional planets. In the symbolism of the wheel, where the hub represents the Intelligible world of the Archetypes and the Unmoving Point at the center represents the Principle, the *outward* direction is necessarily equivalent to the *downward* (cf. p.67 note). The planets beyond Saturn are beyond the rim of the wheel, symbolically in the Outer Darkness, while the three metals are all heavier than lead (which is the heaviest of traditional metals and is also the metal corresponding to Saturn)—in fact so heavy that they decay radioactively under the pressure of their own atomic weight and are inimical to life. Symbolically 'beyond Saturn' and 'below (heavier than) lead' mean the same thing, both denoting the chaotic region outside the bourn of the sacred cosmos, or the inferior psychic domain. Much more might be said on this subject, which could have a chapter to itself, but suffice it here to note that the apparently arbitrary terminological choices of scientists who have no conception of metaphysics may nonetheless correspond to actualities of an order quite outside their comprehension. Language is neither dead nor neutral and operates continually at levels of which most people are unaware—which is one reason that we should be wary of the language we use and not allow ourselves to be drawn into speaking the *argot* of the post-Eclipse world.
6. Whether this theory be accepted or not, the astonishing complexity of single-

many of the problems of the theory, but, of course, destroys it as a substantialist pseudomythos since it no longer even pretends to answer the question of Form, the whole world of animal forms being mysteriously present from the very beginning. Since Forms are no longer supposed to have been arrived at by a sort of accidental version of the Experimental Method, we are back to the ancient question: "Where does Form come from in the first place?" Which, of course, can only be answered by metaphysics.

Nonetheless, even if the pseudomythos should retreat to this position of unconditional surrender, we have no doubt that, so long as the *word* evolution is retained, its position as the cornerstone of substantialist culture, though quite illogical, will remain unchanged.

*

The effects of the introduction of this pseudomythos into Western culture can scarcely be overestimated. C. S. Lewis, in his inaugural lecture as Professor of Mediaeval and Renaissance Literature at the University of Cambridge,[7] makes a strong and well-substantiated case for the contention that between the early nineteenth century and the twentieth there was a change so radical—a transmutation of culture so complete—that it far exceeded all the changes that had taken place throughout the rest of Western history. He argues that between the age of Jane Austen and the very earliest Western civilizations known was a greater kinship than between her age and ours: that they were, for all their differences, together on one side of the divide and we on the other.

We do not have to go so far in order to uphold the view that a cultural change of quite enormous proportions took place during the mid to late nineteenth century. Nevertheless (and bearing in mind that Professor Lewis was only considering the patriarchal Iron Age in the Western world and had not seen the Eclipse), this contention is worthy of serious consideration. Never before had the

---

celled creatures revealed by the electron microscope eliminates gradual evolution as the explanation of complex form, since it is already present in the 'simplest' life forms.

7. *"De Descriptione Temporum"* in *Selected Literary Essays,* ed. Walter Hooper, Cambridge.

world seen a substantialist culture. The changes in literature, thought, and all other areas of life were phenomenal. While the philosophy of substantialism had been with us since the seventeenth century, it had not penetrated the blood and bones of the culture, and then, relatively suddenly, it did. The world was quite rapidly transmogrified into a different place. In many ways, the human soul suddenly found itself cast adrift—cut off from all its metaphysical moorings. And the world itself was (or rather appeared to be) cut off from *its* moorings. The things about us, seemingly severed from their ontological roots in the Celestial Archetypes, became to us but random accidents floating in an aimless, meaningless void. For the first time in history, the mass of educated people, as opposed to a handful of hard-line theoreticians prepared to think substantialism through to the bitter end, were suddenly cast into an accidental, non-Essential cosmos.

From this psychological earthquake flow innumerable consequences, from the neurotic iconoclasm of Cubism, Dada, atonal music, and modernist poetry to the extreme political fanaticisms of the twentieth century. All reflect a world where Form and order, and consequently all sense of proportion, have departed. Nonetheless, as we shall see, the 'modernism' of the twentieth century was by no means uniformly malevolent. The tide of battle had turned decisively in favor of substantialism, but the war was not over, and great things yet remained to be done before the Eclipse closed off all healthy possibilities.

The second passage we quoted from Nietzsche in our first chapter describes the sensation of the nineteenth-century change to a fundamentally (and not merely theoretically) substantialist culture:

> *Who gave us a sponge to wipe away the entire horizon? What did we do when we unchained this earth from its sun?* [8]

Something terrible, something perilous, had happened. What was it? Nietzsche called it the Death of God; but something had

---

8. Note that the imagery used here is *precisely* that of traditional metaphysics: the breaking of a chain or thread, the un-bonding or deracinating of ourselves from our Solar spiritual Source, and, if we turn back to the full passage quoted in our

happened very much deeper than a spread of the vulgar atheism that had been common enough for a century and more. The real disease was the loss of the sense of Essence, the death of the concept of Form. Never again could anyone see beauty as Wordsworth saw it, because now it was just a 'human aesthetic notion', not a golden thread leading back to the Divine.[9]

The 'reductionism' inherent in evolutionism—the deriving of the greater from the less, the reducing of the highest things to banal 'explanations' in terms of the lowest—was mirrored in other spheres, notably in the new 'psychology' of Sigmund Freud, which sought to explain all human aspirations and achievements as mere 'sublimations' of instincts common to cats and dogs, and in the field of sociopolitical theory, where Marx reduces all human culture to an epiphenomenon of economics (we should note that while Marxism may be largely discredited today, its essential legacy remains dominant, and the reduction of culture to economics is now at least as popular on the 'right' as on the 'left').

Of course, the two 'reductionisms' are entirely compatible, since economic motivations are only animal motivations at one remove.

---

first chapter (p.15), the repeated motifs of *darkness* and *cold*. For the deracinated being, cut off from the golden chain that binds her to her Source in the Supernal Sun, is thereby cut off from the solar *light,* which always and everywhere symbolizes pure Intellect (as opposed to the pale lunar glow of earthly reason) and the *warmth* of Divine Love. Such a perception belongs particularly to a sensitive, if perverse, soul finding itself at *the time of transition* between the vestigially Essentialist and fully substantialist eras.

9. Nothing could be more poignant in this connexion than the contrast between the fervent love of beauty of Keats, Shelley, or Wordsworth at the beginning of the nineteenth century and the barren cult of 'art for art's sake' *(l'art pour l'art)* of the *fin de siècle décadents* at its end. The former (including Shelley, whose 'freethinking' was formed by Platonic conceptions) loved beauty in a way that was only possible while its supernatural roots were still perceived, if not fully understood. For the latter the roots had been severed, and the pursuit of beauty had become a barren end-in-itself, a serpent biting its own tail. Desperate as was their emotional desire to pit the Romantic spirit against the surrounding ugliness, they were spiritually hamstrung—or, more precisely, deracinated. The very kinship between the beginning and the end of the Romantic movement makes clearer the impassable gulf that lies between the early and late nineteenth century. It also shows how the bleak anti-Romanticism of the twentieth century was all but inevitable.

In each case we mark the same banality of disproportion, the same explanation of superior things in terms of inferior, as if a great poem or painting were explained wholly in terms of the movements of the artist's finger-muscles, and as if that explanation were considered completely adequate and to have disposed forever of the antiquated notion of 'art'.

We may readily see also how 'evolutionism' lies as the foundation stone of reductionism. Freud needs to explain human behavior in animal terms precisely *because* he is convinced that maid is an animal, existing solely on the earthly plane, and that all her spiritual heritage must be mere 'sublimation' of her animal roots, because these are the only roots she has. Marx's economism shares the same source. We are aware that Marx's earliest work was published over a decade before the *Origin of Species* (being, indeed, a part of the same psychic 'stream'), but the systematic philosophy of Marxism was possible only with the addition of evolutionist doctrine; which is why Marx wished to dedicate *Das Kapital* to Darwin.

Each 'reductionism' also shows the same insensitivity to the question of form, and of each, on its own level, the same question must be asked.

Even if human aspirations and achievements *were* founded on animal desires, why should they take such complex and wonderful forms? Even if human culture *were* a by-product of economics, why should it develop such magnificent and elaborate forms? And even if animals *were* brought about by natural selection, why do they show forth such a plethora of beautiful and needless forms? And *how do we explain those forms themselves?*

Always the reductionist explanation is absurdly inadequate to the thing explained. Human civilization goes infinitely beyond the satisfaction of economic needs, human culture goes infinitely beyond the satisfaction of animal desire, and life on earth goes infinitely beyond the requirements of brute survival. The 'explanations' are all on the level of the wiseacre who, seeing a magnificent palace replete with the finest productions of the architect's, sculptor's, silversmith's, lapidary's, and a hundred other arts, says: "Of course, it's really only a device for keeping the rain off."

But the question of Form may never be asked by the reductionist, for as soon as we admit (as we must admit) that human civilization is driven by a will to express Forms themselves, we shall have to admit that economics is a by-product of culture and not *vice versa,* just as once we admit that the myriad, breathtakingly intricate, and quite needless multiplicity of the Forms of species possess a reason beyond mere utility, modern substantialism is dead.

So, the question is not asked, and the new, demythologized[10] world, stripped of myth by the pseudomythos, is fed on 'explanations' that explain nothing, but drain the life out of everything: reducing the great to the small, the noble to the vulgar, the spiritual to the material, the sublime to the banal. Life becomes suddenly a flatter, colder, emptier thing than we have ever known before, as everything is severed in our hearts from its metaphysical roots—its meaning and the source of its vitality. And to make up for the lack of depth in this two-dimensional world, we must have an ever-increasing agitation of the surface.

The stage is set for the twentieth century.

---

10. 'Demythologization' was a favorite term—and the explicit aim—of the Liberal Protestant school who, precisely in conjunction with the other substantialist movements that followed on the advent of the pseudomythos, set about the project of severing religion from its mythic roots and viewing it on the purely horizontal plane of human history—as, in most respects, did their opponents the Fundamentalists.

Chapter Seven

PSYCHIC DISEASES OF THE TWENTIETH CENTURY

THE EFFECT of the pseudomythos, as we have seen, was primarily that of cutting things off from their ontological roots. This severance is the fundamental cause of the phenomenon known as *deracination* —the general 'cutting off of roots' that we shall see in every area of the post-Eclipse world.

In a very significant essay entitled "The Roots of Plants" *(Les racines des plantes)*[1] the metaphysician René Guénon tells of the Qabbalistic tradition of those who made their way into Paradise and "ravaged the garden" by "cutting off the roots of the plants". The roots of these Paradisial plants grow above, that is, in the Principle itself. Such 'superior roots' are found in many traditional symbolisms and a full, and copiously documented, discussion of the subject may be found in Ananda Coomaraswamy's essay "The Inverted Tree".[2]

This symbolism may operate on a variety of levels, but in every case, 'the severing of the roots', or deracination, means the cutting of an entity from the principle to which it belongs and from which it draws its life and its very being.

It is important also to understand that in the case of a symbolism as profound as this, we are dealing with something of primordial potency. Thus, when the pseudomythos of a false 'evolutionism', in conjunction with the attendant reductionisms discussed in our previous chapter, has the effect of severing, in the heart of maid, every phenomenon—from birds, beasts, and flowers to beauty itself—from its Essential roots, the human world too becomes deracinated.

Of course, the deracination of the natural world is an illusion. Trees and stars and eagles and beauty are *not,* and never can be, cut

1. Translated in Guénon, *Fundamental Symbols—the Universal Language of Sacred Science*, Cambridge, Quinta Essentia, pp. 256-260.
2. Reprinted in Coomaraswamy, Volume I, *Selected Papers: Traditional Art and Symbolism*, ed. R. Lipsey. Princeton University Press, pp. 376-405.

off from their Essential roots. If they could be, they would instantly cease to exist.

The true deracination is not an ontological deracination, which is a metaphysical impossibility, but a psychological, and still more a psychic, deracination in the heart of maid herself.

She too cannot be cut off from her Essential roots. She is still a microcosm, a little image of the universe. She still is what she is because of the Archetype that forms her. None of that can change, whatever she may choose to imagine. But nevertheless, her thoughts, her guiding images, are ritual actualities that take effect primarily on herself.

Living, in her imagination, in a deracinated world in which all things are severed from their Essential roots, she herself becomes deracinated not ontologically, which is impossible, but in many other ways that *are* possible. Just as the microcosm reflects the macrocosm, so maid's great racination, or rootedness, in her Essential form is reflected in a hundred ways in lesser types of racination on the earthly plane. The normal maid is racinated in many different ways: racinated in her family, her village, her country, in her religion, in her relations with her elders and with the stable and benevolent order of the immediate world about her. Her behavior is racinated, reflecting the inner dignity and quiet assurance of a maid who is always conscious of her rootedness in her world and ultimately in Being itself, and who, quite naturally, disdains to say, to do, or to wear anything that would affront that dignity or shatter the harmony of her being.

In a Traditional Society every maid, down to the humblest serving-girl, has something of royalty in her by the simple fact of being a maid—the Axial being: a servant of Heaven and a princess of earth. And even in the lowest form of Normal Society existing before the Eclipse, every maid retained some degree of consciousness of this fact.

After the Eclipse we may see the effects of deracination very clearly. Human beings are torn loose from every possible rootedness, from the local community upwards. All ties, from family loyalties to national loyalties, are undermined by a continuous stream of corrosive propaganda; a cult of 'personal independence' is set in motion, which, while apparently serving the individual, has the effect of cutting each person off from every possible source of support, protection, and comfort, leaving her an isolated unit, completely vulnerable to the mind-shaping, life-controlling totalitarianism of the financial/political complex.

The cults of 'rebellion' and 'independence', contrary to what the naïve are encouraged to imagine, are the perfect instruments for forming a population of mental slaves. Members of traditional communities are hard to control precisely because they have stubborn loyalties; because they have firm criteria for discerning right from wrong and resisting the latter; because they are obedient to the timeless laws of their people; because they believe that eternal truths are more important than the temporary fads being forced on them by their controllers; and because they always have the moral and material support of those who surround them and share their values.

Once those values have been corroded by a specious cult of superficial 'questioning'; once personal loyalties have been rendered worthless by the doctrine that they need only last as long as any given individual finds them convenient; once people have been taught to 'obey nobody' and 'believe nothing': all solid barriers against total centralized manipulation have been broken down. The 'rebellious', 'disobedient', shallow, and deracinated 'citizen' of the post-Eclipse world is in fact the perfectly obedient serf of a mass-media-manipulated tyranny, having neither the criteria nor the support nor the confidence nor the moral fiber needed for any form of real resistance.

Having no landmarks to steer by, she is completely at the mercy of whatever 'suggestions' the system may care to put out, and the more she imagines that she has her 'own ideas' and is not influenced by anything or anyone, the more inevitable it is that her ideas are simply one of the permitted variants on post-Eclipse ideology. For one thing is certain: *no one* has her own uninfluenced ideas. If her ideas are not formed by the primordial tradition, then they will be formed by the substantialist ideology of the modern world.

There are no exceptions: not the present writer, nor the present reader, nor anyone else. There is no genuine question of being 'independent', only a question of *what* we are dependent on. The system that tries to flatter its victims by allowing them to believe that their ideas are 'their own', 'uninfluenced', 'independent', and so forth, is simply a fraud from the beginning. We are all dependent, and always must be. The only question is whether we depend upon Truth or upon falsehood.

Nor is there any question of depending upon 'one's own' falsehood. Necessarily, those who depend on falsehood depend upon the predetermined system of falsehood belonging specifically to the post-Eclipse world. At most they may achieve a minor and insignificant variant of falsehood that they may call their own, rather as a maid in a supermarket may fill her basket with her own selection of predetermined and prepackaged items, all supplied by the centralized retail chain.

We may say, in sum, that the more 'rebellious' a citizen of the late twentieth century is, the more obedient she is. The more she tries to be 'different', 'awkward', 'eccentric', 'warped', 'subversive', 'out for herself', 'nobody's fool', and so on, the more she conforms to *exactly* the type of deracinated flotsam the rulers of the post-Eclipse world are trying to produce. That is why all the images (and sounds) promulgated by the powerful and centralized mass media are finely calculated to promote and popularize precisely these attitudes.

Thus we see that deracination, which has its initial source in a philosophical error, becomes, after the Eclipse, not only a way of life, but the central means of social control.

Deracination, as we shall later see, necessarily goes hand in hand with two other phenomena: *atomization* and *deformism*. Atomization we have already touched upon (without naming it) in the preceding paragraphs. When maids are cut off from the *roots* above them, they are necessarily also cut off from the other people beside them, for the source of true community lies in our common rootedness. Sever us from our roots and we necessarily drift apart, having lost our common ground. The organic bonds and ties that unite traditional peoples (in which term we here include people living in *Normal* as well as in *Traditional* societies) are severed and each individual becomes more and more an *atomized* unit, isolated from all about her and locked in the prison of her own solitude. Certain modern writers have indeed referred to this as the 'essential solitude' of maid: but in fact nothing could be further from the truth. Maid is certainly not *essentially* isolated. It is precisely when she is cut off from her essence that her isolation begins.[3]

We may see this atomization operating at every level in the post-Eclipse world, and we may see how it has become embedded in the social structure as one of its primary means of control.

An interesting parallel may be drawn with the world depicted in George Orwell's *Nineteen Eighty-Four*. In this matter, as in many

---

3. We are aware, of course, that mystics and saints of all traditions have praised solitude, and even in some cases spoken of an 'essential solitude' of maid, but this is something quite different from the atomization of the post-Eclipse world, which is, indeed, the inverse parody of true solitude (which has in any case, only ever been for an élite few and would be intolerable to the majority of human souls who are, and are made to be, social beings).

Many of the destructive tendencies of the modern world are, in this way, inferior or inverted parodies of the higher things, which is one of the meanings of the traditional dictum that "Satan is the ape of God". For example, some of the attacks on the representational art of a Normal Society made by twentieth-century Surrealists and others superficially resemble Essentialist criticism of the same art; but while Essentialist criticism is made from *above*, modernist criticism is made from *below*. While Essentialist criticism wishes art to transcend the material plane and depict the Archetypal realities, modernist criticism wishes art to sink below the material level and depict the chaotic contents of the inferior psychic regions. Again, the nationalism of the post-Renaissance world can rightly be criticized as an untraditional degeneration; but the anti-nationalism or internationalism of the post-Eclipse world attacks nationhood from below, seeking to undermine what has been a healthy form appropriate to a Normal Society and replace it not with more traditional forms but with a wholly deracinated 'global consciousness', which is, in fact (whatever rhetoric it may use to disguise itself as an 'idealism'), nothing other than the world-triumph of the corrosive anti-values of multinational commercialism and the shattering of all normal human loyalties for the purpose of creating the wholly atomized mind-slave.

All these examples are easily understood in the light of the three gunas and their relation to the three types of society—forms that in the Sattwic, or Traditional, Society lead vertically upward, beyond the worldly plane, are replaced in the Rajasic, or Normal, Society by forms that lead horizontally outward and relate wholly to the worldly plane itself (while always, by the very nature of that plane, carrying a reflection of the superior domains). In the Tamasic, or Inverted, Society the horizontal, or Rajasic, forms are replaced by forms once again vertical: forms that lead vertically *downward* into the inferior and chaotic regions below the material; and these Tamasic forms are necessarily inverted parodies of the original Sattwic ones.

others, Orwell's predictions are remarkably correct, but very much less subtle than what actually took place. This is precisely because, not having seen the Eclipse, Orwell was unable to guess to what extent deracination rather than naked compulsion would be used as the means of social control.

In *Nineteen Eighty-Four,* to take an example directly related to the phenomenon of atomization, the Junior Anti-Sex League tried to suppress sex because "loyalty to an individual is disloyalty to the State". In the post-Eclipse world, loyalty is much more subtly broken down by the Cult of Selfishness, while the mystic bonds of eroticism are destroyed not by trying to ban them (which would only lend them greater allure) but by the opposite process of banalizing sex and desensitizing the erotic sensibility by a grotesque and trivializing over-exposure. The so-called 'sexual revolution' of the 1960s has played an important rôle in the development of atomization.

We may note also that the whole concept of "disloyalty to the State", which allows the tyrant and his manipulations to be easily identified, has been replaced by a much subtler and less obvious concept. In place of a 'State' that demands 'loyalty' is an apparently vast and amorphous system of seemingly infinite 'diversity', in which countless 'alternatives' are offered and each individual is encouraged to make her own pick-and-mix selection which she believes is her own, unique, uninfluenced, and rather rebellious personal outlook. In practice, of course, this amorphous system is scarcely less centralized and tightly controlled than the strictest of totalitarianisms. The themes of atomization and deracination run through all the 'alternatives' and 'variations', ensuring that each one produces essentially the same kinds of attitude and behavior (as can be confirmed by watching films made before the Eclipse and seeing how, in contrast to normal people, *all* post-Eclipse people have a strong type-resemblance to each other); and all contribute to the chaos and fragmentation desired in a system of control-by-deracination.

"Loyalty to the State" is precisely what is *not* wanted under the new atomized totalitarianism. Disaffection, cynicism, 'refusal to believe in anything' is precisely what the system desires. A people thus atomized is incapable of gathering itself together into any kind of genuine revolt. 'Movements' and 'issues' rise and fall as the mass media bring them into prominence or drop them into obscurity. Steadfastness of purpose and even duration of memory are all but impossible to an atomized people because their image-sphere is conditioned by the mass media. Even those who do not partake of the mass media are equally conditioned by them, because their entire social environment continues to be manipulated by them.

'Refusal to believe in anything', of course, means in practice 'refusal to believe in anything but the transparent medium of deracination itself'. No one can reject this because no one can see it, and thus disloyalty to everything else becomes total, unthinking, paralytic loyalty to the real State—the state of deracination.

*

Yet we should not imagine that a controlling clique is 'behind deracination'. On the contrary, deracination comes about, as we have seen, as a result of the severance of maid from her spiritual roots. Once deracination becomes the condition of society, it naturally also becomes the primary means of social control. Conformity to the True Order of the Universe, reflected more or less perfectly in the human social order, is the natural condition of maid; and deracination, being the inverse parody of the true order of things, necessarily imposes its own conformity—a strange conformity of apparent non-conformity, but certainly no less rigid for that. The important fact is, that for a social control based, however distantly, upon the Golden Order, we exchange a chaotic, unprincipled, essentially diseased social control that instinctively destroys all that is good and wholesome and promotes all that is corrupt and distorted.

That the various powers behind the post-Eclipse world promote deracination is beyond question; that deracination has become their ideology and that there are enormous financial and political vested interests in the continued erosion of human dignity, the continued atomization of each individual, the continued corrosion of the social fabric, and the systematic prevention of any return to health, is the salient fact of the post-Eclipse world. But to conclude from this that the powers that control the modern world are *behind* deracination would be a mistake. On the contrary, deracination is behind *them*. They too are victims of deracination. Their culture has been destroyed along with everyone else's. They cannot get behind deracination; they are its products. That they believe the vague and absurd 'ideals' churned out by their mass media for public consumption is unlikely, unless they are a great deal stupider than we have any reason to suppose. But since they have quite certainly lost all the ideals that their counterparts in former times possessed— honor, loyalty, love of country and of womanhood—what is left to them but the cynical, isolated, grubby, and ultimately pointless 'self-interest' that they use to control the rest of the population? Politicians in former times may have used such slogans as "England, home, and beauty" to stir the masses, but nearly all of them really believed in such ideals, and ultimately lived for them.

After the Eclipse, for the first time ever, came a generation of controllers devoid of all ultimate ideals. It has been the practice of cynical modernists to accuse all previous ruling classes of being motivated only by 'self-interest'. But they are projecting their own spiritual barrenness on their betters. Self-interest there has always been, of course, and the capitalist ruling class has certainly not been free from it, but 'self-interest' in itself is an interesting philosophical concept. George Bernard Shaw said: "In an ugly world, the richest man can buy nothing but ugliness." What can 'self-interest' consist of in a world devoid of all value?

Earlier generations lived in a world animated by values. It was *within* this, and only within it, that self-interest could have any meaning. A purely atomized self-interest, with no aim or reference beyond itself, was popularized by Marx as the supposed motivation of the historical ruling classes (this, of course, was part and parcel of his substantialist reductionism). But such a phenomenon has never actually *existed* in the history of the world until after the Eclipse.

"England, home, and beauty" may be a shallow slogan, especially when compared with the profundity of traditional wisdom. But nonetheless, such a slogan is not wholly deracinated from that wisdom. It is an appeal, essentially, to the home, or Hestia, which is always and everywhere, like maid herself, a microcosm of the universe; it is an appeal to the nation, as type (however imperfect) of the Golden Order, and to the universal quality of Beauty, which, as we have seen, is the fundamental designation of pure Quality or Essence; nor should it be forgotten that 'beauty' in this slogan quite consciously alludes to English womanhood, and thereby to the universal Feminine.

However shallow might be the application of such a slogan it appeals to fundamental Truths. That is why it works. And those Truths lie at the bedrock of human consciousness, far deeper than mere atomized 'self-interest'. Virtually no one in the English ruling class at the time of the First World War (or much later) did not genuinely believe in the values represented by this slogan, and very few would have hesitated to die for them if called upon to do so.

It is necessary merely to consider that no slogan of this sort— nor, indeed, *any* slogan that appealed to any level of Archetypal profundity or nobility—could possibly be used in the slick, cynical atmosphere of the post-Eclipse world, to gauge how completely that world is severed from its Essential taproot.

Further, one has only to examine the 'ideals' that are supposed to be the fundamental springs of modern political action to see the inescapable barrenness of a deracinated world: ideals such as 'economic growth', 'international coöperation' (to what end—why, more economic growth, of course), 'European integration' (again for the aim of economic growth). The important thing to notice is that "England, home, and beauty" are ends in themselves; reflections of Archetypal reality; shadows, however attenuated, of true Forms. These are things that we may live and die for; while 'economic growth' and so forth, like money itself, are *means* to ends. We want money in order to buy things other than money; we want economic growth in order to achieve things other than economic growth. At least the sane maid does. The pathological miser may treat money as an end in itself, as if it were valuable quite independently of its power of purchasing. The modern political rhetoric likewise treats such *means* as economic growth and international coöperation as ends in themselves, as if they had some absolute value.[4]

---

4. The only other 'ideal', presented in various guises, is 'diversity', which again is not an end in itself, but only a means to the preservation of worthwhile things such as traditional cultures, all of which are in fact systematically destroyed by deracination; while 'diversity' itself is primarily a corrosive used against the remnants of Rajasic Western culture. To 'celebrate diversity' while undermining all culture except deracinated mass-culture is like celebrating houses while murdering their occupants.

The reason is not far to seek. A deracinated society is, by definition, a society stripped of all absolute value, for absolute values lie in the realm of Essence, and that is precisely what the deracinated society has cut itself off from. From now on society can have no true ends, no ideals, no values; it must make do with means, imagining, like the miser, that they are ends in themselves.

Has the deracinated and deracinating tyranny, then, any actual motivation of its own, or is it merely drifting aimlessly, continuing to control and manipulate the population by a sort of reflex action, but with no ultimate purpose? These are matters upon which we can only conjecture, but the works of Nietzsche, who was certainly a more 'advanced' (not to say thoroughgoing and courageous) substantialist than either Marx or Freud, and who may be called the prophet of deracination, shed an interesting light on the question. Having thought through the logic of substantialism pretty much to its ultimate, Nietzsche declares the most fundamental human motivation to be *der Wille zur Macht:* the Will to Power, the pure craving for *power* for its own sake, as an end in itself.

As the fundamental masculine or patriarchal motivation (in a world where the higher motivations that have shaped both feminine and legitimate patriarchal civilizations have been destroyed by deracination) this certainly makes good sense, and is also a fact of observation. Take, for example, the very successful businessman. He sets out with the desire to make money. For what? Presumably in order to buy things: cars, fine houses, perhaps a yacht, or an airplane. He achieves these things, and at a certain point in his career he can afford all that he can actually want. He can dine anywhere he chooses; he can buy more houses than he can possibly live in and more cars than he can possibly drive; yachts and airplanes are his at whim. Clearly the rational man will now retire from business. Its purpose has been served. He has now merely to enjoy the fruits. But does he? In most cases, no. He continues in business, usually to the point where the time he allows himself to enjoy the fruits is minimal. Why? Because business has become an end-in-itself. It is his purpose in living.

But what we must note here is that *money* at this level (and *a fortiori* at the much higher levels from which world-control is exercised) is simply a synonym for *power*. The aim of the businessman is not really to have more money (which is of no *economic* value to him any longer) but to *control* more factories and institutions and thus more people. His activity consists wholly of extending his empire of control. He is motivated completely by the Will to Power.[5]

Is there, then, nothing behind the Will to Power? Is this the final controlling force of the post-Eclipse world, the sole motivation of those who shape, manipulate, and deracinate; who create and enforce the ugly and soulless world-order that is being forced upon the earth's populations?

Consciously, and on the human level, yes. For the deracinated, substantialist world, there can be no true motivations, no values, no genuine ideals, only means disguised as ends (for clearly, power itself is only a means[6]), precisely because means belong to the horizontal plane, the substantial or sensible world, the realm of flux and change and constant dynamic movement, while true ends or ideals belong to the vertical dimension, the Intelligible world, the Essential pole of existence, which the post-Eclipse world has denied. Just as animal species must be held to have 'evolved' purely out of the flux and change of matter, with no underlying

---

5. This is one reason why women, whatever their level of competence (which may often be higher than that of men), tend not to do well beyond a certain level in big business and finance. They lack the essential masculine drive provided by the Will to Power: a Martian phenomenon largely absent from the feminine psyche. It is the corresponding feminine qualities that are needed to redress the balance of late-patriarchal society's destructive power-system, but these cannot operate within a deracinated (and wholly de-feminized) *milieu*.

6. Power (*potens*) is simply the potency, or potentiality, to do something, just as money is simply the latent ability to purchase. Equally, the two senses of 'might' (*Macht*) are ultimately identical—the power, or *might*, to do a thing which therefore *might* or might not be done. It is interesting in this respect that matter, unformed by Essence, is metaphysically defined, particularly by Aristotelians and the Mediaeval Scholastics, as 'pure potentiality'. It is inherent in the 'psychic economy' of substantialism that it must always remain at the level of means, or potentials, never reaching true Actualities.

In this regard, the Tibetan doctrine of Wisdom and Method is illuminating. Wisdom (feminine), of course, belongs to Essence, and Method (masculine) to substance. A substantialist world is, by definition, a world full of method (means) and devoid of Wisdom (true Ends).

Forms, so human action must be motivated purely by *means,* which belong to the world of flux and change, never by true Ends, which, by definition, must originate beyond that world.

Nevertheless, it cannot quite end there. Just as the substantialist explanation of the universe is not the true explanation, so the substantialist account of human motivation is not the true account even of the motivations of substantialists. In the first place there is always an evident dishonesty created by the fact that the human psyche requires Ends and cannot be content with means (which, in any case are absurd in the absence of Ends). Therefore means must continually be *disguised* as ends by empty rhetoric and pseudo-idealism.

But beyond this, and far more important, the human psyche is *always* motivated by Ends whatever may be the appearance and the conscious state of affairs. When true Ends are cut off, inverted parodies will necessarily take their place, and this, of course, is precisely in keeping with the nature of a Tamasic age.

The very vehemence with which the deracination of every aspect of life is pursued by the controlling powers of the post-Eclipse world; the very rancor with which every vestige of human dignity, decency, and charm is attacked and mutilated, are evidences of motivation working at a far profounder level than can be consciously understood or acknowledged by any substantialist. The *apparent* and acknowledged motivations for the direction of the post-Eclipse world are too naïve to consider seriously; the underlying drive of the Will to Power is real enough—it is a masculine-substantialist motivation for the controllers of a masculine-substantialist world, and, as far as it goes, it is very effective. But maid does not live by substance alone, and beneath the flat, de-Essentialized surface of the post-Eclipse world lurk the true human motivations in reverse (which is why the post-Eclipse world is termed an *Inverted* Society).

Whereas a Normal Society is guided unconsciously (as a Traditional Society is guided consciously) by a love of the Archetypes, of Form and Beauty, an Inverted Society is guided, equally unconsciously, precisely by the hatred of those things. The Archetypes can never really leave the human mind, nor can it remain indifferent to them. If it does not love and conform to them, then it must hate and seek to despoil them, and in everything the post-Eclipse world does, this is the salient feature; it is the connecting thread, the true family likeness, between all its 'varieties' and 'alternatives' which may often seem to be very different and may frequently be bitterly opposed (since a deracinated society thrives on discord). The one thing they all have in common is a hatred of Form and Archetype.

Everywhere, we see the drive to distort every possible form, to disfigure and mock the sacred human image with every variety of clownish dress, adornment, and mutilation. Whatever the reasons put forward, the underlying motivation is the hatred of the human image itself. Again, femininity is attacked for a variety of social and political reasons, but behind those utilitarian excuses lies a true hatred of the Feminine. Whatever represents 'home and beauty', whatever may racinate a soul on any level, must be destroyed, and the 'reasons' given for that destruction are of very little consequence. Reasons can always be found.

In whatever direction we turn we shall find the same thing. Everything that is beautiful or graceful, anything that is sane or ordered, anything that is romantic or kindly must be twisted, distorted, mocked, vilified, and destroyed. In every direction we see the same aspiration to the low in place of the high, to the chaotic and disordered in place of the harmonious, to the diseased and degraded in place of the upright and pure.

Here lies the most fundamental motivation of the post-Eclipse world.

Just as a Normal Society continues to turn about the axis of the Archetypes, an Inverted Society turns about the axis of the Antitypes—of the inverse parodies of true Form. No other motivation, indeed, will suffice for the deeper levels of the human psyche. Nothing that does not relate to the world of pure Form—albeit in an inverted manner—can truly touch maid's soul or give her the underlying will to create a social reality.

To state the same thing in a more 'mythic'—but certainly no less true—language, we may say that the real 'leadership' of the post-Eclipse world is not human at all, but literally 'diabolical'; and that whatever its conscious motivations, an Inverted Society dances always to a tune played from below.

Deracination, then—the state of being cut off from Essence—necessarily leads beyond itself to *deformism,* the positive perversion and distortion of earthly forms and the invocation of dark parodies of the Archetypes in every sphere of human existence.

Chapter Eight

ART NEO
AND THE RESURGENCE OF LIGHT

IT WILL be noted that between our last two chapters lies something of a gap in our narrative. From the promulgation of the pseudo-mythos in the mid to late nineteenth century, with its inauguration of a fully substantialist and demythologized culture, we moved directly to the complete deracination of the post-Eclipse world nearly a century later.

There is a reason for this 'jump'. Deracination was the direct result of the final mythic dislocation of the West by the pseudomythos, but it was not, at least in the all-enveloping form encountered after the Eclipse, the *immediate* result. To examine deracination immediately following our examination of the pseudomythos and its attendant reductionisms was the best way to make clear the process that occurred in its broad outlines. It is now necessary to step back and examine what took place in the intervening years: that is to say, in the twentieth century up to the point of the Eclipse in the early 1960s.

As has already been made clear, the world of the pre-Eclipse twentieth century in the West was still a Normal Society. Despite the massive psychological changes following the propagation of the pseudomythos, it was still typologically at one with the rest of the post-Renaissance world. What we have is a *demythologized* world that is still not *deracinated*.

The reason for this is partly that the phenomenon of deracination took some time to permeate through every level of society, and partly that the positive spiritual forces that had been at work in society throughout the period of the Normal Society were still active. The pre-Eclipse twentieth century was, indeed, a battlefield on which beneficent and malevolent forces were ranged against each other, fighting for supremacy in many areas of life.

In order fully to appreciate the situation, it is necessary to pose another question which many readers may already have raised in their own minds. Since the inevitable movement of the historical cycle is from Essence to substance, from quality to quantity, from feminine to masculine, were not the disasters we have chronicled—the Eclipse, atomization, deracination, deformism—predestined occurrences which could not have been otherwise?

The answer is that the process of historical decline and consolidation is certainly inevitable, but it may proceed along either or both of two paths, which we may term the Stream of Light and the Stream of Darkness. The Stream of Light constitutes those influences that favor the development of what we have called the late fruits of the historical cycle, in other words, decline along the Stream of Light would mean that, while consolidation was certainly taking place, it was taking place in the most beneficent possible way, with the favorable developments inherent in the lowest phase of the cycle being encouraged to the full. Conversely, decline along the Stream of Darkness would mean an exploitation of all the most malevolent aspects of consolidation and the complete suppression of its more favorable potentialities.

In practice, before the Eclipse, the historical decline took place neither exclusively along the Stream of Light nor exclusively along the Stream of Darkness. The nineteenth century, for example, developed both the malevolent potentialities of that particular historical stage and the great cultural and other fruits that were inherent in it.

We may say that the Stream of Light and the Stream of Darkness were intertwined throughout the Normal period of history, sometimes strongly opposed, in cases where one or the other must prevail in some particular, and also acting upon each other's work, since the conditions created by movements within either stream necessarily affected the operating *milieu* of the other.

However, with the propagation of the pseudomythos, the conflict between the Stream of Light and the Stream of Darkness entered a new phase. For the first time, the total victory of the Stream of Darkness became a possibility, and in the early twentieth century movements were initiated for the complete deracination of the human world.

These movements took place not primarily in the spheres that a modern person would perhaps expect. There were certainly movements in the political sphere, connected with the inversion of the pyramid; but from the metaphysical point of view, political developments are always of secondary importance.

The most significant movements took place in the sphere of art and culture; particularly the former—and this is entirely to be expected when one remembers that, from the metaphysical perspective (which necessarily governs all others), the most important aspect of any phenomenon is *form*—and, as we have seen, while the explicit ideology of a substantialist culture is to deny the importance of form, its underlying motivations always concern the inversion and distortion of form.

The early twentieth-century movements in the arts, then, following the substantialist impetus created by the pseudomythos, and instinctively working out its inner spiritual implications, launched an attack of a sort that had never before taken place anywhere in the world: *a direct and conscious assault on beauty itself.*

Before the early twentieth century there had been people who were indifferent to beauty; there had been industrialists and others who had held that practicality was more important than beauty, and that where the two came into conflict beauty must be sacrificed. Such people earned the undying contempt of artists everywhere. But never before, anywhere, had there been people who actually opposed beauty *per se:* people who actually believed that beauty was to be avoided and the ugly or the shocking pursued as an end in itself. Far less had there been artists who founded their art upon the rejection of beauty. Yet this was precisely what happened in the early twentieth century with such movements as Cubism and Dada.

When the young T. S. Eliot wrote, in *Prufrock:*

> *Let us go then, you and I,*
> *When the evening is spread out against the sky*
> *Like a patient etherized upon a table;*

he was deliberately inverting the beautiful imagery of the Romantic school and seeking to replace it with an image that would shock and disturb.

In its day this was new; but after the Eclipse the almost permanent aim of artists, advertisers, television program-makers, and just about all who communicate with the public is to shock and disturb in precisely this sort of fashion. The futility of such an exercise is evident. By now people are so inured to shocks of every sort that very little will disturb them (at least consciously), and the psyche of the post-Eclipse public is like a jaded drug-addict taking ever more massive doses of ugliness and grotesquerie to achieve ever diminishing results.

However, having followed our exposition up to this point, and having understood the importance of form in general and of beauty in particular, our reader will, we trust, be able to understand precisely why this treason against beauty *was,* and *is,* and always must be, genuinely shocking and disturbing, and why the shock involved is not of a kind to give one a mildly pleasurable thrill, but of a kind that should genuinely horrify anyone who understands what it really signifies.

We have said that the pre-Eclipse twentieth century was demythologized but not deracinated,[1] but it is clear from the above that deracination had already taken hold of many individual psyches. Indeed, by the mid-1920s, and increasingly thenceforward, deracination became the permanent condition of large portions of the intellectual and artistic 'élite' of the Western world;[2] though it is important to understand that this deracination, real as it was,

---

1. It is interesting to note that T. S. Eliot, one of the earliest poets to introduce deformism into his work (as shown in the example above), was clearly conscious of the issues involved. *The Waste Land* confronts the problem of a demythologized and potentially deracinated world, and his work from that point onwards is always concerned in one respect or another with the remythologization of the modern world. Much of his problem was that he was conscious of the destructive nature of demythologization while caught in the snare of the deracination that followed from it. A study of his work from this perspective would be of very great interest, epitomizing as it does both the malaise and the will to recovery of the pre-Eclipse twentieth century.

2. It would take us beyond our brief to examine this phenomenon in detail, but we may remark that the 'stream of consciousness' school of literature marks a high point in the development of atomization, shifting the 'action' of the novel entirely within the isolated consciousness of the individual and being by nature inimical to the organic bonds of social life. Partly in reaction to this and similar atomizing tendencies, many writers of the 1930s adopted Communism, a creed that focuses

could not be by any means as deep and thoroughgoing as that which prevailed in the post-Eclipse period precisely because the deracinées of this period were still surrounded by a broadly racinated society and were filled with residual racination from their own childhoods. It may be said with complete accuracy that the most 'advanced', opium-smoking Bohemian of the 1920s, and even the most degenerate beatnik of the 1950s, was nowhere near as deeply deracinated as any suburban bank manager of the 1990s.

---

all worth exclusively within the social sphere and rejects what it terms "bourgeois individualism". Needless to say, the socialism of Marx is no answer to the problem of atomization, being based on precisely the same fallacies—for 'collectivism' (as the very term implies) is not founded on the organic and ultimately microcosmic wholeness of the Social Order, but merely regards society as an aggregation or collectivity of individuals, and is therefore ultimately no less atomized than the most extreme forms of individualism.

There may seem to be little common ground between Christian Fundamentalism and literary Communism, but in one respect they are very similar. They are both examples of a very common tendency within the substantialist world: the tendency to react against some substantialist movement without possessing the intellectual equipment to reject the error on which it is founded. Thus Fundamentalism challenges demythologizing liberalism with an equally demythologizing literalism, and Communism challenges atomizing individualism with an equally atomized 'collectivism'.

We also have here a clear example of what may be called the 'Tamasic dialectic': the process by which such 'unprincipled oppositions' (by which we mean oppositions founded on no authentic intellectual principle) may set up a rhythmic movement leading the conceptual life of the modern world to ever lower levels. The thesis and antithesis formed by the two terms of such an opposition are frequently resolved into a synthesis compounded of the lowest elements of both terms and discarding the higher elements of each.

In the present case we may observe that the refinement and delicacy of the 'stream of consciousness' school and its cognates was too rarefied to become a permanent feature of modern, and especially post-Eclipse, literature, while the 'idealism' (albeit misguided) of Communism could not possibly withstand the all-corrosive cynicism of a wholly deracinated world. However, the literary and general 'intellectual' ambience of post-Eclipse society is strongly infused with an amalgam of the crude, sloganized politicism of the sub-Marxist outlook (together with many of its reductionist nostrums, which continue to form the basis of most post-Eclipse political thinking, both 'left' and 'right'), and the near-autistic atomization of the 'stream of consciousness' school, while discarding completely the 'idealism' of the one and the aesthetic refinement of the other.

However, this is only one half of the story of the earlier twentieth century. Despite the steadily increasing deracination and atomization of the 'intellectual élite',[3] a strong countermovement was forming in the aesthetic and cultural spheres, although one wholly devoid of any intellectual underpinning and therefore established on very unstable ground.

The invasion of everyday life by the machine in all its forms was one of the salient characteristics of the earlier twentieth century, and one seized upon as serving its purposes by the Cult of Ugliness, which grew naturally out of the psychological deformism of the deracinated pseudo-élite. William Morris had taught, in the later nineteenth century, that the machine is ugly. His answer was to retreat from machine culture into an arts-and-crafts movement little adapted to the conditions of the present phase of history. While Morris said in effect: "The machine is ugly, therefore let us abolish the machine", movements such as Cubism in the early twentieth century gleefully inverted the argument, saying, in effect: "The machine is ugly; we cannot abolish the machine; therefore let us embrace ugliness." This argument had a certain persuasive force, although it was essentially only a rationalization—a rationalization of the rapidly growing love of ugliness and absurdity *for their own sake,* which is the cardinal feature of the deformist mentality and is so clearly central to the 'culture' of the post-Eclipse world.

What, however, may perhaps seem surprising is that the twentieth century also produced an aesthetic strongly opposing the Cult of Ugliness and the growing deformism of the demythologized world—and that it did this quite specifically in the arena of machine-production.

The movement now generally known as 'Art Deco' was precisely an answer from the Stream of Light to the aesthetic problem of the machine. Before proceeding further, we should like to define a little more closely exactly which movement we have in mind. Art Deco is a term applied retrospectively (a variety of terms, such as 'streamline

---

3. This 'élite' may be said to be the inverse parody of a true intellectual élite and to perform the precise opposite of the function performed by such an élite in a Traditional, or Sattwic, Society—and of course has no connexion whatever with transcendent Intellect.

moderne', were used at the time), and, though it is usually taken to mean the particular movement we have in mind, it is both too broad and too loose for our purposes, sometimes including barren and blockish forms that belong rather to the *opposite* movement, to the expression of formlessness and deformism.

We therefore use the term 'Art Neo', and let us define precisely what we mean by it. By Art Neo we mean those aspects of Art Deco that are most generally associated with the name—the theatrical, upward-aspiring forms exemplified in the interior of the original Daily Express building in London and the Chrysler building in New York. It is a style that makes exhilarating use of geometrical line and curve, yet is never divorced from the human spirit; that places solar imagery at the heart of much of its design; and contains a continual upward (Sattwic) and outward (Rajasic) thrust. It will be seen that the blockish designs sometimes included in the term 'Art Deco' are the very reverse of Art Neo, by their very mass and gravity exerting a Tamasic downward pull, and everywhere negating the human in favor of the alien, the cold, and the lithoidal. This blockish style took over from Art Neo in the sphere of architecture after the Second World War and reached its zenith in the hideous tower blocks of the 1960s, though it had been present throughout the inter-war period as the Stream-of-Darkness opponent to Art Neo (often under the name of the 'International Style'). It may be called the apogee of the movement of consolidation in the sphere of design—that movement not yet having passed beyond material consolidation into the stage of disintegration and chaos. Although this stage had, of course, already been reached in many areas of the 'arts', it took longer for the disintegrationist movement to reach the areas of public design—this, as we shall see, is the main thrust of post-Eclipse design.

Having defined Art Neo, we may see how it permeated every sphere of public and industrial design, so that, as the Art Nouveau movement of the early years of the century was displaced by the products of the machine, instead of the immediate triumph of the blockish and the inhuman, foreseen triumphally by the early deformists and expected with pessimistic but equal certainty by the waning representatives of the old aestheticism, there intervened a new movement from the Stream of Light, a new fruition of the positive tendencies of the Cycle, in the form of a style of design that embraced the machine without subordinating the human spirit to it; which made a new, uplifting, glorious, humanized world out of what could have been the Wasteland of the Machine Age.

More than this, Art Neo shows us and future generations that there *is* a way forward. If industrial design is ugly, inhuman, cheap, and garish, we know for certain, as we could not have known if Art Neo had not had its brief but glorious flowering,[4] that it *need* not be so. That ugliness is *not* inherent in the machine. That if hideousness is foisted upon us, it is a deliberate (albeit often unconscious) choice of the designers, not an unavoidable necessity.

But the term 'Art Neo' (unlike 'Art Deco') may be applied to a much wider range of things than those comprised in the world of design. The popular music of the 1920s and (especially) the 1930s is Art-Neo music, its sharp syncopations and lilting melodies corresponding precisely to the angles and curves of visual Art Neo.

C. S. Lewis, in an essay entitled "High and Low Brows",[5] demonstrates the impossibility of distinguishing between 'high' and 'low' art near to the time of its production and points out that much of the art now regarded as of the finest quality was in its own day considered vulgar and insignificant. He suggests it is quite possible that a time will come when "our age is known to posterity not as that of Auden and Eliot, but as that of Buchan and Wodehouse". What is curious here is that having cited two poets as representatives of the art that is considered 'serious' in the twentieth century, he then cites two *novelists* as their possible counterparts. This is obviously because, on the face of it, there is no such thing as a popular poetry in the twentieth century (as there was in the nineteenth). In fact, however, there *is* popular poetry in the pre-Eclipse twentieth century—but all of it is set to music. The lyrics of the Art-Neo music of the 1920s and '30s—and its successors up to

---

4. Art Neo flourished between the 1920s and the early 1960s. While it was strongest in the early decades, there was very much a vibrant 1950s continuation of Art Neo, even though 'International-Style' influences—no longer so called—were gaining ground in many areas.

5. In *Selected Literary Essays* edited by Walter Hooper, Cambridge.

the time of the Eclipse—are the popular poetry of the twentieth century; and the great poets of the century may well be not Auden and Eliot, but Cole Porter, Lorenz Hart, and Noel Coward.[6] It is by no means unusual for great poems to be songs written to music, although the tradition died out in the eighteenth and nineteenth centuries. Many of the great Elizabethan lyrics were written to music, as was much of the Greek anthology. The very word 'lyric' means a song sung to the accompaniment of a lyre. But unlike the great Greek and Elizabethan lyrics, we do not believe that the great twentieth century lyrics ever should be, or ever will be, severed from the wonderful music to which they are indissolubly married.

Just as the novel, and the romantic movement in music, painting, and poetry, allowed the expression of areas of human sensibility untouched by earlier and higher arts, so the popular song of the twentieth century, and the film, have explored new areas of the soul only appropriate, and only accessible, to this late age. And all these things belong to the great artistic movement that we term Art Neo.

The great art of the twentieth century is a democratic art in the best sense of that term; it belongs, we may say, to the lowest common denominator of humanity; but it does not seek to reduce humanity to its lowest and least noble elements (as does post-Eclipse culture). Its general aspiration is always upwards, always toward what is high and pure and good in the human spirit, and even where individual productions may take a cynical or an immoral turn, that is largely negated by the broad thrust of the movement of which they are a part. And what is most notable about the Art-Neo movement

---

6. These names are quoted primarily for purposes of evocation. While there certainly are many great individual writers in the Art-Neo lyrical anthology, as with the sixteenth century lyricists and the Greek Anthology itself, there are many small gems by writers little known and immortal for only one or two of their verses. The flowering was that of a period rather than an individual flowering. And as with those other periods of poetic fecundity, the Art-Neo lyric explores many areas—the love lyric in its various forms, satire, idyllic pieces, evocations of many primary human sentiments in ways unique to this charming *genre* of the 'democratic' period, often with a revived and vital use of the literary *conceit* that had become rare in the Romantic era.

whether in song or film or decoration, to a later and more degraded age, is always its unassailable *innocence*—an innocence that is not in any way false, but corresponds to the true nature of humanity and which, even when corruption is abroad among the élite, continues unassailed among the great and sound mass of the population. This was the case in the pre-Eclipse twentieth century, and only ceased to be the case when a massive assault upon the innocence of the people was launched through the mass media, the educational system, and every organ of public propaganda after the Eclipse. The innocence of the people is a bulwark against every kind of corruption. That is the true value of cultural democracy in a declining age, and it shines through every production of the machine-and-democratic art *par excellence,* Art Neo. Shines through until it is ruthlessly and systematically destroyed by the forces of post-Eclipse darkness.

*

We begin, then, to form a picture of the missing period in our account. It is not simply one of a steady decline from a demythologized society into the deracinated, atomized, and deformist society depicted in our last chapter, rather we see a resurgence of Normal, or Rajasic, form, that is all the more remarkable in view of the complete collapse of any intellectual or mythological underpinning for such a resurgence. This phenomenon not only testifies to the great persistence of the love of racinated form and Archetypal reality in the human soul, but also gives justifiable cause for hope in the future. Beyond doubt, the Art-Neo movement, in all its forms, demonstrates that the romantic flowering of the nineteenth century had not exhausted the good fruits of the historical Cycle.

The only question to be asked in this connexion is whether the democratic art of the twentieth century was a thing so late and low and shallow-rooted that the four decades of its expression (from the beginning of the 1920s to the Eclipse in the early 1960s) represented all that it had to offer; whether it had not completely exhausted its potentialities in that brief period, leaving nothing further to be unfolded but the chaos and inversion of the Last Days, of which the Eclipse marked the beginning.

At this point of historical proximity, we cannot know for sure whether this is the case or not. But the present writer ventures to suggest that it is not—that the Art-Neo stream has still much that is good left in it, and that its development, rather than having run its natural course and expired, was untimely paralyzed, but not necessarily killed, by the triumph of the Stream of Darkness at the time of the Eclipse.

If this *is* so, then two things must follow. First that the end of History is not yet at hand, and secondly that the inversion and darkness brought on by the Eclipse is not final and must come to an end with a new resurgence of Normal civilization. For as long as there are fruits to be gleaned, as long as there is more in the Cycle to be unfolded, the Cycle cannot yet end.

But it also seems clear that there are certain preconditions for any resurgence. The Normal civilization of, say, the 1950s was living on the dwindling inheritance of earlier times. Its intellectual darkness was all but complete; its demythologization was total; insofar as it could be the scene of a continuing Normality and even of a revival of certain aspects of Normality[7] it could only be by a blind inheritance of the forms of higher phases of culture, quite unassisted by the smallest intellectual perception of their true meaning.

That inheritance is now largely disintegrated under the systematic corrosion of several decades of inversion and perversion. If a resurgence is to take place, it will be necessary for at least a minimum of metaphysical understanding to return to at least a portion of the Western populations. The intellectual darkness of the modern world must be enlightened to some small extent if a racinated, Normal world is to return.

It is to this end that a book such as the present one is directed.

---

7. For the 1950s were indeed the time of a rather beautiful revival of femininity and of a democratized version of the domestic virtues, and many people who are attempting to re-racinate themselves, by, among other things, a systematic self-nourishment with the films of the Art-Neo period, find the films of the 1950s actually *more* racinating than those of the 1930s.

Chapter Nine

THE LANGUAGE OF FORM

WE HAVE spoken of the deracination[1] of the post-Eclipse period, and we must speak also of the cure for this disease—a cure ultimately for civilization as a whole, but in the first instance for those few individuals who will have the courage to lead the way and to begin, within themselves, the psychic movement that will lead to resurgence. For the return to health, if it is to take place at all, cannot be merely theorized or advocated. It must be *lived* by those who believe in it. It must be brought into being on this earth by the ritual action of an entire way of life. For if the chaotic forces of patriarchy-run-mad are to be defeated, certain people alive today must give their lives for it. Not give their lives in death, but give their lives to the abundant joy and heroic achievement of re-racination in the midst of a world that is wholly deracinated.

We shall return to this in due course. But in order to understand the cure, we must first understand the disease.

We have already considered deracination, with its attendant atomization and deformism, at some length from the theoretical point of view. It is now necessary to consider their practical effects and workings in the post-Eclipse world.

When we said that in order to understand the cure we must first understand the disease, we were not speaking merely figuratively. The effects of deracination, when it takes hold of a society, are very

---

1. We use the term 'deracination' as a single designation for the threefold disease of Tamasic culture, deracination being, as it were, the starting-point and salient characteristic. However, we should understand that the Three Poisons of the Tamasic Society are *deracination, atomization,* and *deformism.* These three correspond precisely to the three gunas: *deracination* is the cutting off of the superior roots, the isolation of the human world from its essential rootedness in the upper or Sattwic direction; *atomization* might be called 'horizontal deracination', the cutting off of one human being from another in the horizontal, or Rajasic, direction; while *deformism,* the orientation toward the inverse parodies of form that lie in the inferior regions, and the embrace of ugliness, grotesquerie, and deformity, is oriented wholly in the Tamasic, or downward, direction.

similar to the effects of a disease upon an individual body, or of an epidemic upon a community. Like a disease working within an organism, deracination, atomization, and deformism rapidly take hold of all the different functions and expressions of a culture, corrupting and despoiling each one until there is no aspect of the diseased society that is not riddled with the disease and its effects.

Before the Eclipse, Western society was an organism infected by the disease, but still fundamentally healthy; its antibodies were still fighting the disease and full recovery was still a daily possibility. After the Eclipse, Western society is an organism whose immune system has collapsed and in which the disease runs rampant and unchecked in every direction, corrupting every avenue of social expression.

In certain areas this is obvious. In others it is perhaps, at first, less so. There is little difficulty for most healthy people in seeing the disease in the way post-Eclipse people dress; in the raucous and degenerate popular 'music'; in the garish and exploitative nature of many magazines, films, and television programs; in the crude immorality that is promoted by every organ of public communication; in the cult of selfishness that is propagated everywhere; in the breakdown of trust and of the sense of community; in the increasing 'acceptability' of foul language; and in many other of the most salient everyday features of post-Eclipse society.

What is subtler and less obvious until one begins to understand these matters more fully is that *every* aspect of post-Eclipse culture is a carrier of the same psychic disease. One area, for example, whose importance is frequently underestimated is that of design. The design of a post-Eclipse automobile, telephone, plastic kettle, set of music-playing equipment, or any other item of everyday use is as diseased as the nastiest popular song or most blatantly vile picture-magazine.

In order to understand this, we must realize that no object of human design and manufacture is morally or philosophically neutral. Every made object is *saying* something. Design is not and never has been mere meaningless embellishment. In the traditional Sattwic Society the design and ornamentation of every object of daily use had a spiritual and metaphysical reference. Scholars such as Ananda Coomaraswamy have commented at length on the profound and beautiful *intellectual* significance of ancient artefacts. As this author put it: "The 'history of design' remains an absolutely sterile exercise when abstracted from the intellectual life that can alone account for the facts of design."

Exactly as we should expect, the language of design as used in Traditional, or Sattwic, cultures expresses upward-leading truths: spiritual and metaphysical realities. The ornamentation and form of every object of daily life carries a meaning that is a constant 'reminder' to the user of her Celestial origin and of the Path of Return. Just as every craft is a Way for the craftsmaid, an Initiatic path of reintegration, so the 'products' of her craft, from a pot to a chariot to a palace, contribute to the psychic health and wholeness of the user and of all who behold them.

In the Normal, or Rajasic, culture, the intellectuality of the Language of Design is progressively forgotten. The ornamentation of an object is eventually reduced to 'mere decoration' in the minds of both its producers and its users. Design has no conscious object other than to be pleasing and convenient. Nonetheless, as we have pointed out before, whatever its *conscious* aims and intentions, the human mind is always conditioned by the Archetypes; and so long as it has not been poisoned or inverted, it is *positively* conditioned by them. So, in the Normal culture, while the conscious intellectual underpinning of design is progressively lost, design itself continues to represent healthy forms. Its direction is now 'outward', or Rajasic, as opposed to the metaphysical or upward orientation of the design of artefacts in a Traditional Society; but insofar as this healthy outward development is untainted by any perversion, it will necessarily remain true to the Essences of all true form, and thus will always reflect 'secondarily' the upward direction.

From an eighteenth-century carriage to a 1958 Chevrolet; from powdered wigs and face-patches to the New Look of Christian Dior; from an early Georgian mansion to the Empire State Building —all these are representative of the same design language: that of the Normal, or Rajasic, culture of the modern West. It is a language referring essentially to this world and neither to the superior states above it, nor to the chaotic regions of inferior psychism below it. Nevertheless, since the forms of this world, so long as they are not corrupted, are always reflections of the eternal Forms, the design of the Normal culture is never wholly severed from superior principles, even though its attachment to them may be largely unconscious.

As we have said, no object of human design is morally or philosophically neutral. The design of Sattwic cultures is consciously intellectual. It deliberately expresses a spiritual thesis that is as clearly 'readable' to any cultured person as the words in a book. The intellectual content of design in Rajasic, or Normal, cultures is no longer conscious, but it is not one whit less real. Every line of every artefact made in the Rajasic period expresses a thesis. The exact *nuances* of that thesis change somewhat between, say, the eighteenth century and the Art-Neo period, and the precise nature of those changes would make an interesting and valuable study in itself. For our present purposes, however, we need merely note that the broad outlines of the Rajasic thesis remain the same: a this-worldly emphasis (which from the standpoint of design-language—now divorced from conscious intention—is as true of religious art and design as it is of secular), but a concentration upon the healthy, the beautiful, the noble, and the elevating aspects of earthly life—as indeed, is no more than natural when maid is designing for her own use and pleasure. And since all that is healthy and noble and beautiful in earthly things is also closely connected to the celestial Archetypes (indeed, what do the terms 'health', 'nobility' and 'beauty' mean in terms of form other than fidelity to the Pure Forms?), the Rajasic culture is always 'secondarily' Sattwic.

What, then, do we find in the design-language of the Tamasic period that followed the Eclipse of the early 1960s and reached its fullest intensity some two decades after? In every area we find the rejection of nobility, followed inevitably by the rejection of beauty and health. Design, at its best, is marked by a slickness and garishness that negates any possibility of the noble or the uplifting. At its worst—which increasingly becomes the norm—it aims quite consciously at being odd, outlandish, lopsided, and abnormal. A plastic jug-kettle, for example, is a deliberate negation of the Archetype of a kettle, rejecting every element that links it to its ontological root. The slick soullessness of the telephone kiosks that wantonly and quite unnecessarily displaced within a year the beautiful red Art-Neo British 'phone box' shriek of the emptiness and impoverishment of the post-Eclipse world.

Much post-Eclipse design uses the excuse of 'cheapness' and 'convenience' for its hideousness, but this *is* nothing more than an excuse. Given the same budgetary limitations, the same technics, and the same materials, the inspired designers of the Art-Neo period would have produced very different objects. Objects that would uplift the soul rather than filling it with a sense of hollowness and worthlessness. Design is, before all else, a *language,* expressing a *thesis:* and the thesis of post-Eclipse design is the cheapness, ugliness, and worthlessness of life, and ultimately the chaos and the meaningless glare and babble of the inferior psychic regions.

Cheapness itself is a symptom. The very willingness of the deracinated post-Eclipse person to fill her home with slick plastic in order to pay a little less money is symptomatic of a very terrible change. An Art-Neo wireless set is, before all else, a piece of furniture in polished wood and gleaming metal or bakelite. It cannot be any-thing else, because the home before the Eclipse—every home, from the greatest to the humblest—is still vestigially a Temple of Hestia, and its mistress still a Priestess of the Hearth Fire. The remembrance of this *Mysteria Domestica* may be extremely remote, yet it is still a living thing that governs human actions at a very deep level. Only that which is solid and good and worthy of the dignity of the Temple of the Home will be admitted within it. A radiogram that is to occupy a prominent place within the home *must* be a noble and beautiful piece of furniture, else it cannot occupy that place.

So much hardly needed to be stated before the Eclipse. It was simply obvious to everyone, to manufacturer and advertiser and mistress of the house alike. No one could possibly imagine that for the sake of a marginal financial saving any sane person would desecrate her home with the sort of soulless artefact that fills every shop selling wireless equipment (or anything else, of course) in the last decade of the twentieth century.

Such a thing was not even thinkable before the Rajasic period passed into the Tamasic; and it is only necessary to contemplate this phenomenon for a few minutes—those who have eyes to see and souls to sense with—to understand very intensely what a terrible thing has befallen the Western soul over the course of these few short decades.

Nonetheless, we must reiterate that the Cult of Cheapness, although it is certainly a significant part of the malaise of the post-Eclipse world, does not and cannot provide a true explanation of the soullessness of post-Eclipse design. It is true that a racinated person *would not* put cheapness before every vestige of dignity and beauty in buying appliances for her home, but even if cheapness *was* for some reason the overriding consideration in design; even if racinated designers were faced with *exactly* the same material and financial considerations as the designers of the late twentieth century, deracinated design would not and could not be the result.

Conversely, however much money a deracinated designer may have at her disposal, however much may be lavished on materials and design values, the result is always deracinated design. Design is, we repeat, a *language,* and one that, after the decline of the intellectuality of the Sattwic ages, operates largely unconsciously. In other words, the designer of the Rajasic period cannot do anything other than produce worldly-but-racinated design, and the designer of the Tamasic period cannot produce anything other than deracinated design that is poisonous to the soul. The very fact that these designers (as well as their 'consumers') do *not* know what they are doing makes them all the more powerless to do anything other than what their 'culture' directs them to do.

The corollary of this is that *nothing* produced in the post-Eclipse period is free from the psychic disease of deracination and deformism, and this extends to every possible area of expression. For example, some people say that while most post-Eclipse television programs are clearly poisonous, some are quite harmless and innocent. Now, even if this were true of the overt content of the programs (a very much more unlikely state of affairs than one may realize), the disease still manifests itself in a hundred ways of which we may not at first be fully conscious—in the typography used for screen-lettering, in the colors and forms used for display material, in the clothes worn by the announcers and other visible personnel, in the camera-angles, in the use of music and sound, in the very gestures and speech cadences employed for the commentary (invariably per-formed by people specially trained for the job, and therefore more 'advanced' in the deracinated human manner than the average person). Apart from its obvious, conscious content, every television program is sending a thousand signals into the mind, most of them unnoticed and therefore 'subliminal', but certainly no less effective for that.

Let us be clear that we are certainly not postulating some 'conspiracy' on the part of the television companies (indeed, such a conspiracy would be relatively crude and ineffective compared to what is actually happening). What in fact is taking place is a much subtler and much more all-pervasive process based upon the quasi-organic nature of psychic disease. The disease of deracination and deformism acts just like a material, organic disease. It follows out its own laws and its own logic. Anyone who has contracted the disease becomes a carrier and helps to spread the disease to others, without necessarily having any conscious intention of doing so. At the lowest level this is the case with everyone who, having been persuaded by her surrounding ambience to wear deracinated clothes, then becomes part of the surrounding ambience that persuades others to do the same. At the higher levels, everyone concerned with the design of artefacts, the making of television programs, the production of advertisements, and every other aspect of the 'culture' of the post-Eclipse world (and remember that, to succeed in their competitive fields, these people must reflect the latest and most 'advanced'—which is to say most deracinated—approach) is continually inject-ing the poisons of deracination into the surrounding culture, even as she herself imbibes those poisons *from* the surrounding culture.[2]

---

2. This poisoning includes not merely the *positive* inculcation of deformist images, but also the *negative* destruction of all healthy images, either by distorting and parodying them, by juxtaposing them with deformed images (which actually enhances the deformity of the latter while co-opting the former into the economy of deformism), or in general by overlaying them with the implicit cynicism of the Tamasic mentality and placing them firmly within the quotation marks of 'the past', thus denying them all effectiveness. The Tamasic regime says, in effect: "You are permitted unpoisoned images provided you regard them as 'things of the past', wholly devoid of any effect in your current life"—rather as Communist regimes

And as it is precisely her job to be *'au fait* with the latest trends' and even (which is not particularly difficult once one gets the 'feel' of a particular aspect of deracinated culture) to anticipate them, she becomes a part of the organic process, helping the disease to develop, step by step, into ever deeper levels of deracination, atomization, and deformism.

If all this should seem a little abstract, let us suggest a very practical experiment. Watch any part of a children's program from the 1950s, *Watch with Mother,* say, or one of those programs that have charming, well-spoken schoolgirl announcers. Now watch any announcer from a current children's television program that you may have supposed to be 'innocent'—observe everything, the color, the style, the sounds, the entire *manner.* Do you still think it harmless? Compare the psychic health, the order, the serene harmony of the one with the slick neurosis and spiritual impoverishment of the other. Consider how one is (quite unconsciously) designed to heal and racinate the soul of a child, and the other to disrupt and cheapen it. We have made this demonstration to many people over the years, and not one has failed to perceive the truth of it when confronted by the stark contrast between the two cultures. This exercise alone is sufficient to make clear in the very depths of one's being the

---

used to forbid worship in churches but preserved the churches themselves in immaculate condition as museums.

This Tamasic totalitarianism, or deformist imperialism, is also evident in the strangely hysterical attitude that a supposedly 'open' and 'pluralist' system adopts toward what it terms 'cults'. The term 'cult' in this new usage means 'any group of people who attempt to define reality'. The real difference between a 'cult' (Bad) and an 'alternative' (Good) is that 'alternatives' are permitted variants within the Tamasic system, while 'cults' attempt, successfully or otherwise (and their success is usually severely limited by the fact that they are themselves deeply conditioned by the Tamasic world), to declare psychic independence from the system. The Tamasic world as a whole, being the primary definer of reality, is (to apply its own terms impartially) a super-cult, and it automatically attacks all lesser, rival cults that might impinge on its monopoly of reality-definition. The salient mark of a 'cult' (as opposed to an 'alternative') is that it attempts to *secede* from the surrounding ambience, cutting off poison-sources such as the mass media and supplanting them with its own self-defined 'culture'. As we shall see, secession is the *only* way of freedom from the system, and that system is impelled by its inner logic to seal off any means of escape.

meaning and reality of psychic poisoning.

And in general, as soon as we begin to look at the things of the pre-Eclipse period not through the quotation marks of 'belonging to the past', which the post-Eclipse world uses to neutralize their effect, as soon as we realize that they represent a norm and a standard against which the post-Eclipse world can be judged, the insanity and disease of the post-Eclipse world becomes so glaringly apparent as to be the most obvious—and indeed, the only really significant—thing about it.

*

We wish to make it clear that this is *not* in any sense an attack upon the technical or medical advances of the post-Eclipse period. This mistake is easily made by those who have only a superficial understanding of the Essentialist criticism of the modern world.

On the contrary, the technical advances of the Tamasic period belong essentially to the Rajasic period. That is to say, they are products of the momentum built up over the three centuries and more of Normal civilization. Small, powerful computers and all the other advances of recent years would have happened *whether or not* the Eclipse had taken place. There is nothing in them that belongs to the cultural degeneracy of the period in which, by an historical accident, they have emerged. Nothing, that is, except their outward casing—the language of design with which they are surrounded—and this has nothing whatever to do with their inherent nature.

If microchip technics had been developed a little after the First World War, we should now be able to find computers from the 1920s and '30s in beautiful Art-Neo designs, as lovely as those of the wireless sets of the same period.

It is clear, then, that the technics themselves are essentially Rajasic, and, indeed, are possibly the only area in which the Rajasic current of the Normal world continues into the Tamasic post-Eclipse period. Thus, not only is Essentialist criticism of the Tamasic culture *not* an attack on the technics that have come about during that period, but, conversely, the apologists for the Tamasic Society cannot claim those technics as its saving virtue, as they so often try to do. For when challenged to find something worthwhile about the post-Eclipse period, most people will cite some technical or medical advance, since very few people genuinely find its culture acceptable.

But we must go further and say that the very existence, success, and continued progress of the technical arts is really no more than a residue from the Rajasic period. The work involved is based upon a discipline of thought and action that is scarcely to be found in other areas of post-Eclipse society, and it is perhaps for this very reason that dominance in technical matters is gradually passing to the Far East where less atomized and more racinated forms of social order still partially survive.

Technical advance, far from being something that belongs to the Tamasic world, is a legacy from the Rajasic world; and one that will eventually become exhausted if no return to a more Normal form of society takes place.

*

There is one further aspect to deformism that we must consider. We have seen that every element of design, speech, or image, every form-aspect of a human culture, has an intellectual content: it is *saying* something. This was consciously true in the more intellectual and metaphysical climate of the Sattwic ages, and less consciously true—but no less true—in the Rajasic and Tamasic periods.

But the form-elements of a civilization are not merely *saying* something. They are *doing* something. Again, in Sattwic societies there is a conscious awareness that every act is a ritual act, every object a ritual object. The fact is consciously known and consciously utilized, that every symbol has an effect on the psyche; and every traditional object, from a pot to a garment to a house, is consciously designed to integrate the human psyche with the cosmic totality and to elevate it toward the Divine.

In Rajasic societies this consciousness rapidly dwindles, but the faithful adherence to the earthly plane in its healthier aspects means that human life and expression continues to be a ritual of integration. Its symbolic forms still promote wholeness and health in the psyche.

In the Tamasic Society, however, this is reversed. Its symbolism and form-language are deliberately perverse, disruptive, and disintegrative. Their effects are to atomize the soul from its surroundings and to fragment it within itself. The entire tendency of every aspect of the culture is corrosive, and this corrosion is a ritual act that disrupts the soul; a repeated invocation, that, with every seeing or handling of a deracinated object, every exposure to deracinated sounds and images, every contact with deracinated individuals, furthers the process of psychic disintegration.

The idea that one can 'understand what is wrong' with modern objects, television programs, and so on, and therefore be able to expose oneself to them without harm is as fallacious as to imagine that because one understands the workings and knows the effects of arsenic one can therefore ingest it with safety.

Tamasic forms are effective ritual invocations. They are, in the truest sense of the term, black magic; and they achieve their effective results quite irrespective of whether the victim is conscious or unconscious of their nature, is coöperating or resisting, willing or unwilling.

Modern people are apt to say that something is 'only symbolic' as if that meant that it was devoid of power. In fact, symbols are the most potent effective forces in the world, and while the forms, clothes, objects, sounds, and images of a Tamasic culture cannot be called 'symbols' in the true and sacred meaning of that word, they are certainly anti-symbols: the inversion and desecration of all the symbolic realities that have shaped human life and destiny over countless millennia, and as such have a power for evil that is truly incalculable.

It will be asked at this point: since most people have no choice but to accept some degree of exposure to the forms of the post-Eclipse Tamasic culture, what, if anything, can be done to prevent psychic disruption? Is there any protection against the disintegrative process, any cure for its effects, either for the individual or for society as a whole?

Certainly there is both protection and cure for the individual, and, we believe, in the longer term, for society as a whole. Let us proceed to consider these possibilities.

Chapter Ten

SECRETS OF THE IMAGE-SPHERE

PSYCHIC POISONING, as we have seen, is not just a figure of speech. It is a stark reality, and one that pervades the post-Eclipse Western world in its entirety, manifesting through the design of the manufactured environment and the objects of everyday use, no less than through clothes, music advertisements, and broadcast programs.

Given the all-pervasive nature of deformism, its saturation of the culture at every level and in every area, it may seem an impossible task to free oneself from it and to create a healthy and nourishing environment in the midst of this soul-choking atmosphere.

But it is not impossible. The human spirit, the feminine spirit, cannot and will not admit defeat.

Let us begin by considering precisely how the creation of a deformist society works. We can see that each broadcast program, each manufactured artefact, and so on, is a brick within the entire edifice of the deformist whole. But exactly *where* is that whole constructed? Where does it exist?

The simple answer is: in the mind. First in the various individual human minds that have been exposed to the various symbolic expressions of deformism, and then in the group, or social, mind formed from the aggregation of those individual minds. Remember, all the symbols of deformism are statements that can only be interpreted by *consciousness* and the only unit of intelligent consciousness, according to the modern mentality, is the human mind. Of course, the modern mentality is wrong, and there *are* other and much higher forms of consciousness than the individual human mind. But these higher forms of consciousness have nothing to do with deformism. So at the level at which the deformist project takes place, the human mind *is* the only unit of consciousness, and all that it does has its being in and through that consciousness.

Now every human consciousness exists in what we may term an *image-sphere*. By image-sphere we mean the form-world in which a consciousness exists: the things it sees, the things it believes to exist, the things it thinks about—these *are* the world to that consciousness.

The deformist culture attains its ends by controlling the image-spheres of its individual subjects, and thereby controlling the group image-sphere of the whole society. With modern methods of mass communication, it has become possible for small groups of people or moneyed interests to manipulate the image-sphere of an entire civilization in a way that has never been possible in the past. In the past (that is, in the Rajasic period), the group image-sphere was like the city of London rather than a modern planned city. It consisted of various elements drawn from various times and places, some of it virtually unchanged since matriarchal times, some of it remaining from early patriarchal times, some of it instilled by the present dispensation of the moment, and much of it lying at various points in between the ancient and the modern. It was not a whole, integrated image-sphere based on pure principle and directed upwards, as was the image-sphere of the purest Sattwic ages. But it was mostly a mixture of relatively healthy elements. This is in the nature of a Rajasic age, but in any case nothing else would really have been possible.

Only with the advent of means of communication capable of pumping a set of images derived from the minds of a small, highly conditioned 'élite' into every home in the land, has it been possible to create and impose a completely artificial image-sphere upon whole populations. The total and arbitrary control of the group image-sphere of an entire civilization is something new in history. Its very possibility is a technical novelty; but even so, it can only be effective with a wholly deracinated people, who are easily prized loose from all the inherited images and realities that any traditional people retains within itself.

The total, artificial control of the image-sphere has become a reality. But it is still true that the individual image-sphere—*your* image-sphere—can only be controlled if you allow it to be.[1]

---

1. This being the case, it may be wondered why virtually everyone, with negligible exceptions, allows her image-sphere to be controlled by the centralized machine of the Tamasic culture. The fundamental reason, as outlined in Chapter 7, is precisely the cult of 'rebellion', 'aggressive individualism', and constant 'questioning', all of which, while superficially appearing to grant greater freedom to the individual, in fact cut off every escape-route from centralized control. The only way to get a tune out of one's head is to sing another tune, but if one is too anarchic and

The question, then, is: how can one regain control of one's individual image-sphere?

First of all, one must become acutely conscious that the human psyche[2] is an extremely sensitive thing. It is affected by everything it

---

undisciplined to adhere to the rules of melody then one will always be dominated by the prevailing tune.

The pretended 'diversity' of the Tamasic Society, with its countless apparent 'alternatives', all of which are but variations on the theme of deformism, both disguises the monolithic nature of the Tamasic tyranny and plays upon individual vanity to keep the soul enslaved.

Only by a wholehearted acceptance of Rajasic forms can the image-sphere be freed from Tamasic control. The Tamasic culture, however, encourages its members to be too 'clever' to be wholehearted about anything. Rajasic forms are quite acceptable to the Tamasic Society provided they are not accepted purely and innocently for what they are, but as part of an ironic eclecticism of a fundamentally Tamasic nature. In this way does the Tamasic Society neutralize all attempts at escape not founded on a full intellectual understanding of the situation.

An interesting illustration of this was provided by a university undergraduate who wished to throw off the chains of Tamasic conditioning. She said that she wished to adopt a fully 1950s style of dress, but would be too embarrassed to go to University dressed in this way. She said that she would have no embarrassment at all about attending university with a shaven head and a ring through her nose (she did not *wish* to do this, but it would not have embarrassed her)—nor would she be embarrassed about wearing fully 1950s dress if she *also* wore a ring though her nose (again, she did not *wish* to do this, but knew that the ring would avoid embarrassment).

This demonstrates some very important points: 1) How embarrassment is employed to keep people in obedience to the unwritten Rules of Tamas. 2) How everyone actually knows what the rules are even though she generally imagines that there are no rules and that she is 'expressing herself' rather than following a set pattern. 3) How any Rajasic form (such as 1950s dress) is permitted and welcomed by the Tamasic world provided, *and only provided*, it is mocked by some deformist element. In television programs this is frequently done by supposedly 'unusual' (but in fact tediously predictable and compulsive) juxtapositions. In bourgeois houses, if there is elegant traditional furniture or decor, it *must* be juxtaposed with plank bookshelves, block-mounted pictures, and the like. Indeed, the twisting, parodying, and placing into cynical quotation marks of healthy images is a vital part of the deformist vision.

2. Modern English is extremely poor in vocabulary describing the non-material parts of maid, and one is constantly faced with the choice between using an established modern term rather loosely, and burdening the reader with yet another 'specialized' term, so many of which have already been necessary for the explication of our

sees, hears, and experiences. The *Bhagavad Gita* tells us that we become what we think about and that the soul after death is assimilated to the things upon which the mind dwelled during life. The Bible says: "As a man thinketh in his heart so is he". This same wisdom is to be found throughout tradition.

Modern people are generally very careful about what they put into their mouths. They will not normally pick up any interesting edible thing from the street and swallow it; but no similar caution is exercised over what they put into their *minds,* and, indeed, the concept of *mental hygiene* is one that takes a considerable adjustment in our whole way of thinking. Everything in the Tamasic world is strongly against it. Everything encourages us to think that we can see, hear, and mentally ingest anything without any particular consequences; and that we *should,* therefore, make a practice of mentally ingesting whatever comes our way.

Actually this attitude is extremely recent. Even a few short decades ago, most people (especially women) exercised some caution over what they watched and read, whom they associated with, and what kind of talk they listened to. They were intuitively aware that it was entirely possible to poison themselves by mentally ingesting the wrong sorts of thing. Elizabeth Barrett Browning's caveat against the damage to the psyche that can be done by harmful reading matter was well understood by her contemporaries:

> Behold!—the world of books is still the world. . .
> . . . the wicked there
> Are winged like angels; every knife that strikes
> Is edged from elemental fire to assail
> A spiritual life [3]

We may note how this poem, which was published two years before *The Origin of Species* and still on the other side of the great watershed

---

theme. When we use the word *psyche* in this chapter, we are really referring to what the ancient and mediaeval West termed the Sensitive Soul, and in particular the faculties known as *vis phantastica* and *vis imaginativa* ('fantasy' and 'imagination'— but those words as used in modern discourse are probably more misleading than helpful) [*vide* C. S. Lewis, *The Discarded Image*, pp.161-165].

3. *Aurora Leigh*, Book I, lines 748-753.

of the pseudomythos, still speaks, albeit 'poetically', in terms of the four elements and the traditional cosmos, still knows that unseen things are more real than things seen, and that psychic and spiritual dangers are, to say the least of it, every bit as real as physical ones. Few 'intellectuals' of the demythologized twentieth century would have written in this vein, but most people before the Eclipse still retained an instinctive sense of psychic self-protection: an understanding that unclean things could poison the psyche and that one should exercise caution over what one allowed into the Sensitive Soul[4]—and no doubt also a sense that the psychic power for good or evil that had been wielded in the past by books was relatively small compared to the power of the much less intellectual, but much more psychically pervasive, media of film and television.

This natural and instinctive caution has been broken down by a steady stream of propaganda emanating from a degenerate mass-media establishment whose whole *aim* is to poison.

So our first step, before we *do* anything, is to begin adjusting ourselves to the idea that the psyche is a delicate and highly sensitive mechanism. Or to use a different metaphor, it is like a garden—what grows there is what has been planted there. At present, the money-power of the Tamasic Society, with its mass media, its advertising agencies, and its various permitted and promoted 'alternatives', has complete control over what is planted in the individual and collective image-spheres. If we wish to reclaim control of our image-sphere, we must learn to *cultivate* it—to take conscious control over what is allowed into it, what is nurtured and encouraged, and what things it must be protected from.

The cultivation of the psyche and its image-sphere involves two things: planting and nurturing racinated and whole images, and excluding deracinated and deformed ones. The psyche (or Sensitive

---

4. Where intellectuals from the late nineteenth century onwards acted consciously against this instinct and purposefully invited morbid images and experiences into the psyche, they were acting deliberately 'against the grain' (the title of the first notable book of the 'decadent' school, *A Rebours* by J. K. Huysmans, means exactly that) and willfully subordinating their self-protective instincts to their mental theories. These same theories have, since the Eclipse, been gradually and systematically used to break down the self-protective instincts of entire populations.

Soul) *feeds* on images—and 'images', in this case, must be under-stood in the broadest possible sense, as including not only visual forms, but sounds, gestures, tones of voice, vocabulary, clothes, and a thousand other things.

Where can racinated images be found? The first answer to this, for ourselves at present, must be: in the Rajasic world that immediately preceded the Eclipse. This is the first source of *assimilable* images. We may go back further and find truly traditional or Sattwic images, but they will not change our image-sphere, partly because they are too far from the everyday workings of our present consciousness and partly because they do not challenge the Tamasic world *on its own level*. Even if we do assimilate such images, they will not actually transform the image-sphere. We are certainly not speaking against the use of such images, only warning that they will not be effective used on their own.

The transformation of the image-sphere—the driving-out of the Forces of Occupation from the psyche—must be effected by the use of the image-sphere of the Rajasic world closest to us in point of time.

How do we gain access to this Rajasic image-sphere? Fortunately and indeed we believe providentially, in the fullest sense of the word, the motion picture came into being several decades before the collapse of civilization, capturing the image-sphere of the late Rajasic Society—that is, of the Art-Neo restitution period—in nearly all its main aspects, in a form easily and thoroughly assimilable and psychically very powerful. It is also providential that, owing to its 'popular' nature, the film has preserved for us almost solely the regenerative aspects of that period: atomization, deracination, and deformism being, at that time, chiefly intellectuals' diseases.

The film, then, is one of the main instruments in the recapturing of the image-sphere. Using it skillfully and consciously, we may saturate the psyche with racinated images and begin to create a free and whole image-sphere.

By the *skillful* and *conscious* use of the Art-Neo cinema for this purpose we mean several things. In the first place, there is probably no better instrument for the recapturing of the shattered image of true femininity, but some people will fear that since these images come from the patriarchal era they must imply a patriarchal sub-ordination of women. There are many possible answers to this problem, but the simplest and most practical is to point out that the approach of Aristasia, to which the present writer belongs, is to watch the films and racinate the psyche within the context of an all-female group and a very largely all-female image-world that acts as a potent counterbalance to the patriarchal nature of racinated cultural elements from the Rajasic world. Undoubtedly other solutions can be found. The point is that the problem *is* soluble and should not be allowed to stand in the way of the reclaiming of the image-sphere.

Furthermore, we shall find in these films images of feminine magnificence—of the glorious and powerful qualities of femininity that belong to the feminine itself, and are not merely imitations of masculine strengths—that cannot possibly be found anywhere in the inherently anti-feminine Tamasic world. Indeed, the whole concept of the 'subordination of women' in the Rajasic period, while not untrue, is a very limited and one-dimensional notion, which sacrifices to crude, sub-Marxist sociopolitical reductionism all that was true and beautiful in the image and experience of femininity in this period, and concentrates all worth in masculine criteria of money and power. We shall find in these films the true majesty of femininity in its many forms, and as we learn to see them truly, we shall see with both joy and anguish what a treasury of feminine glory has been lost, forgotten, and plowed under in the last few decades.

This must lead us on to wider considerations. How, precisely, *can* the Art-Neo cinema be used to effect a transformation in the image-sphere? Clearly simply watching the films is not in itself sufficient. After all, they are freely available and widely viewed in the post-Eclipse world without making the smallest difference to the collective or individual image-spheres. In the first place, the films must be watched as part of a wider program of racination, and the intake of Tamasic material must be curtailed. We shall discuss these matters shortly. But more immediately, a *willed act* must be taken to see the films in a racinating way.

The reason racinated films have no noticeable racinating influence on those who watch them from the perspective of the Tamasic world is that they are, so to speak, enclosed within a neutralizing sheath that prevents them from having any actual effect. This 'sheath' consists, first of all, in placing the films firmly in 'the past', so that their very age is sufficient in the eyes of the majority to prevent their having any 'relevance to the present' and therefore any effect on the way one perceives the world. Then the films are enclosed within further layers of distancing reactions—nostalgia, condescension, cynicism, and, in general, the seeing of the film through the distorting-lens of post-Eclipse attitudes.

In short, one is unconsciously taking the Tamasic world as the standard against which the film must be judged, whereas, if we are to free ourselves from the grip of that world, we must take the Rajasic world represented by the film as the standard against which the Tamasic world is to be judged.

To do this, we must remove the film entirely from the patronizing quotation marks of 'the past' and understand that it represents Reality here and now—and, indeed, the *only* glimpse of legitimate human reality to which we have access. We must see through the trick of 'relevance' and 'currency' which the Tamasic world and its money-power employs for the purpose of dominating our image-spheres. The image-sphere is filled with the things promulgated by the mass media, news services, and advertising agencies. They are what we surround ourselves with mentally because they are happening 'now', and therefore are 'real'. All they are, in fact, is the selection of manufactured reality that the system chooses to present us with. And because the system is all-encompassing in a way that no previous system has ever been, there is no alternative to accepting this unless we choose our images from areas over which the present regime has no control: in other words, from 'the past'.

The *image* of a public figure such as a film star, and the individual person upon whom that image is based are two quite different things. The Tamasic world surrounds us with deracinated images which we are encouraged to accord a special immediacy because their prototypes are alive (and, of course, therefore obedient to the prevailing, manipulated ethos). In fact no image is inherently 'realer' than any other, *and we may select any group of images we choose to populate our image-sphere.*[5]

And yet, while we have said that no image is 'realer' than any other, we must realize that this is speaking on the purely 'horizontal' plane of the imaginative possibilities of the image-sphere. On the 'vertical' or spiritual plane, the images of the Rajasic Art-Neo cinema are much realer in the Essential sense—they are nearer to true Reality because they have not wholly lost their connexion with the fundamental Archetypes that underlie all being.

In watching the films, then, we must let go of the materialistic and superficial assumption that the passage of time is any criterion of reality, and know that in the most important sense what we are seeing is far *realer* than the Tamasic world about us, and represents the standard by which that world must be judged and the model from which our own re-racinated world shall (in part) be built.[6]

---

5. There is a certain irony in the fact that, for all the Tamasic propaganda machine's fraudulent prattle of 'freedom' and 'choice', this realization is the *only* one that can give the individual any real freedom or control over her mental environment, which is precisely why the Tamasic system uses every subterfuge and distraction to keep her locked into its centrally controlled image-sphere.

6. We shall no doubt hear the weary old argument that the Art-Neo film is an unrealistic and idealized representation of the society in which it is set. In reply we should say that we are not, for our present purposes, interested in social realities, but in *images*. And we are very happy to compare like with like—that is, Rajasic films with Tamasic films, in which the Tamasic world has every opportunity to depict its *image* of itself rather than the social reality. We would say that the image is, if anything, rather nastier than the reality, which at least is modified by some remaining resistance from human goodness. Indeed, this is the salient point about the two types of society. One sets up an image *above* its present attainment—more beautiful, more stylish, more kindly—with which it saturates its image-sphere and to which it aspires. The other sets up an image *below* its present attainment—darker, more chaotic, more violent and atomized—with which *it* saturates its image-sphere, and to which, whether it admit it or not, it aspires, and certainly grows continually closer.

In fact, far from constituting an objection, if Rajasic films represent Ideals, surely that is precisely what we want, since we are using them to 'stock' our image-sphere and the more 'ideal' the material with which we stock it the better. Indeed, the Art-Neo film could profitably be a great deal *more* idealized than it is; however, we must bear in mind that the 'idealism' of the Art-Neo era is accidental rather than principled—that is to say, based on healthy human taste rather than a conscious desire to represent the Archetypes, and we may be grateful to Providence that such a fine image-sphere of Rajasic idealism has been preserved for us so miraculously in the amber of the film.

Chapter Eleven

SECESSION AND THE HESTIA

THE FUNDAMENTAL building block of civilization is the home. A single family home is a society in itself. A few homes make up a hamlet. As we add more we get a village, a town, a city. Each of these is an extension of the home.

Every traditional home, be it an igloo, a grass hut, or a stone house, like maid herself, is a little cosmos. The central pole of the teepee is the World Axis: its conical form reiterates the symbolism of the pyramid discussed elsewhere. The hearth fire in a house corresponds to the sun in the cosmos and the heart in maid. Traditional rituals of the foundation of a home make explicit (and ritually 'actualize') these correspondences and the vital link between the microcosm of the house, the macrocosm of the world, and the other microcosm of maid.

In patriarchal societies, men came to dominate the *Agora,* the public world (from the Greek word for 'market-place'—hence *agoraphobia:* 'fear of public places'), but the *Hestia,* the home world, remained primarily the province of women. The Hestia is, in fact, where much of life—the very heart of life—takes place. Our home is, indeed, as the idiomatic phrase so tellingly puts it, the place *where we live*—wherein our very existence is centered.

In the Tamasic age, the Agora is, at least temporarily, beyond redemption. Any notion of 'political reform' is inevitably far too shallow to be of value, since it must necessarily leave the poisons of deracination, atomization, and deformism, which are *not* primarily political phenomena, untouched.

Only by re-creating a racinated *life* in its totality can anything of value be achieved, and this can only be done in the Hestia. The way forward must lie in the creation of racinated *homes* as sanctuaries from the disease of late patriarchy. Such racinated homes must form a society between themselves, even if they are separated by physical distance, and the society so formed must, as far as possible, *secede* from the surrounding deracinated culture, creating a new culture and a new social order.

Some will ask whether 'retreating' in this way can be of any real value, but we must first note that the very concept of such a strategy as a 'retreat' is founded upon the acceptance of the patriarchal doctrine of the Primacy of the Agora. The idea that only that which takes place in the Agora is of any importance has been growing steadily through the patriarchal period, until, with the super-patriarchy of the post-Eclipse period, women were encouraged to feel that the life of the home was of no importance whatever and to center their own lives, like men, upon the Agora. Thus the Hestia, as a center of social life, was virtually eliminated.

From a feminine perspective, on the contrary, the Hestia is the most important part of society. A society with Hestia and no Agora would be, it is true, a truncated society; but a society with Agora and no Hestia is no society at all.

The development of a rudimentary Agora within a seceded society must remain a problem for the future; but for the present, a model social order founded on the aggregation of racinated Hestias is infinitely preferable to life in a poisoned Agoracentric society.

Chapter Twelve

WHAT THE FUTURE MAY HOLD: THE ARISTASIAN EXPERIMENT

IN THE thirteen years since the first publication of this book, nothing has happened to make us wish to change or add to our diagnosis of current Western civilization. It continues on precisely the course indicated in the book, at much the speed that was to be expected.

Two long-term tendencies, however, have become apparent in this period. One is the beginning of a weakening of the West in relation to the East in economic and (more gradually) military terms. This will fluctuate over the coming years, but we may be fairly certain that the era of the absolute dominion of the West is coming to an end.

The other tendency is the rise of a force in the world that is completely opposed to the materialist, secularist settlement of the current 'world order' and has declared upon it war to the death. We refer to radical 'Islamism'.

At the beginning of the decade in which this book was first published, Francis Fukuyama, deputy director of the policy planning staff of the U.S. State Department, famously announced "the end of history". With the fall of Communism, we had, in his words, reached "the end of history as such: that is, the end point of mankind's ideological evolution and the universalization of Western liberal democracy as the final form of human government."[1]

At the time, to those who follow only the material externalities of events, his words seemed plausible, but it is now abundantly clear that he spoke far too soon.

What are the long-term possibilities of the two tendencies mentioned above? The strengthening of the East in relation to the West portends very little if the East continues, as it does at present, simply to ape European ideologies (whether liberal-capitalist or socialist). But what if, at some point in their rise, Eastern nations begin to ask themselves why they are still mimicking the ideas of their former conquerer? The eastern nations were violently (and

---

1. Francis Fukuyama, "The End of History?", *The National Interest*, Summer 1989.

often not wholly) plucked out of a late-Sattwic phase and thrown into a late-Rajasic into which some Tamasic elements, with greater or lesser success, were in some cases introduced. Witness the strange amalgam that is contemporary Japan.

Meiji Japan, rather than await the invasion and humiliation visited on China, initiated, from the 1860s onward, an aggressive and highly successful mock-Western Rajasic order. During that time, Lafcadio Hearn, who lived in Japan and adopted Japanese nationality, wrote that Japan's Westernization was founded on the principle of jiu jitsu—using the enemy's strength against him—and that the heart of Japan remained unchanged and was only employing an exterior Westernization for its own ends.[2] Atomic devastation, unconditional surrender, and foreign reshaping (even the Emperor was 'de-divinized' by American decree) has changed all that.

The West has reshaped the East by three things: by force, by threat of force, and—in many ways most potent of all—by the hypnotic effect of its own superior material success, which has convinced Eastern peoples that the only way to prosperity is to 'think Western'. What happens when all three of those factors cease to operate? Will the Eastern nations seek to recreate their own way? A true Eastern Rajasic? There are straws in the wind, such as the Chinese rehabilitation of Confucius, who until recently was harshly vilified in the name of European Marxism. Time alone will tell whether, and in what form, such a movement may take place.

Radical 'Islamism' is a worldwide phenomenon openly hostile to the 'end of history' liberal democracy that is still accepted as the only legitimacy by the so-called 'international community'. Let us be clear that, while it is branded as 'conservative' and is certainly intolerant, this is a new form of Islam which in many ways rejects tradition and may quite properly be compared to the rigorist anti-traditional movement of Christian Fundamentalism, which similarly opposes obvious modernism while having essentially modernist roots itself.

This, however, is not the last word on the matter. The fact that an anti-traditional force (perhaps necessarily) provides the 'spearhead'

---

2. Lafcadio Hearn, *Out of the East: Reveries and Studies in New Japan* (1895), Ch. VII.

in breaking down secularism, does not mean that that force would ultimately prevail if secularism were defeated.

Now by the defeat of secular liberalism, we are not necessarily referring simply to Islam. If it became a great enough threat, radical Islamism could force the West to reassess itself. Decades of Tamasic ideology have softened the West to the point where it is not ready to defend itself against a really serious threat. To pose the most central test: how many current Westerners believe in their society and its vision strongly enough to die for it? How many Islamists do? To resist a serious threat, the West would be forced to rethink its current shallow values, or else face defeat.

Each of these possible shifts might indicate that the true 'end of history'—that is, the end of the current historical cycle, with all the Rajasic streams played out and only the final Tamasic residues left—may not be yet upon us.

Whether any of them might be called 'good' from the point of view of a reader of this book is highly debatable. What seems likely is a hardening of patriarchy as part of a retreat into the late Rajasic. This is by no means certain, of course. Restitution of any kind is impossible to predict.

Whatever the future, we are bound to ask if there is a course open to those who embrace the Feminine Essentialist approach outlined in this book—one that embraces feminine spiritual values without falling into the errors of late-patriarchal 'feminism' or the spiritual aberrations of the 'New Age' movement.

Among the first fruits of the Feminine Essentialist revival—which long predates this book—was the grouping known as Aristasia. This is a community that regards itself as an all-feminine nation, which rejects the Tamasic developments of the late twentieth and early twenty-first centuries and seeks to create a feminine Rajasic culture on earth in the current era.

Aristasia actively encourages the worship of God as Supreme Mother and was instrumental in starting the website *A Chapel of Our Mother God*, which at the time of writing is coming close to receiving 1,000 unique visitors per day. The publication of *The Gospel of Our Mother God* in book form marks an important point in the advance of Déanism.

Gradually, other congregations are beginning to emerge, focusing on Our Mother God, not as a psychological phenomenon, an allegory of 'women' or 'the earth', nor as a 'neo-pagan' demigod, but as the One True God, Creatrix of Earth and Heaven.

What is unique about Aristasia is that it is actively attempting to create not merely a congregation, but a society; a society that breaks free from the Tamasic aberrations of the last four decades and founds itself on a basis of Amity in place of atomization and of the Golden Order of traditional maternal hierarchy.

Aristasia has such an extensive philosophy that one can hardly begin to discuss it without using its own special terms (look up 'Amity' in the online *Encyclopaedia Aristasiana,* for example). This is important because the English language has been shaped and molded by rationalist Rajasic terminology over three centuries and a new terminology is required in order to discuss many things in depth without re-explaining oneself in a hostile language on each occasion.

But Aristasia is not just a philosophical discussion-group: it is a way of life based primarily upon the Aristasian household and also increasingly on virtual interaction by means of the Internet.[1] As we have attempted to explain in this book, it is not just how one *thinks* that is important, but how one *lives*: how one shapes one's image-sphere and casts off the misshaping that has been imposed upon it.

A return to innocence and Amity within a feminine community is the Aristasian mission. It will not appeal to everyone and is not intended for everyone (it is limited to women to begin with). However, as a deeply Tamasic society goes forward into the uncertainties of a new century, we feel that Aristasia will *be* the path for some, and for others may be the light that shows them their own path.

---

1. One of the technical changes of this century will be the increasing encroachment, in many spheres of activity, of 'virtual worlds' upon what has currently become a way of human life more physically based than any before it. Holographic conferencing, in which participants across the globe may be virtually in the same room is already a reality, though not yet widespread, and the eerie mixture of virtual and real in which a pilot at a screen in Arizona may fly real (and deadly) missions in Afghanistan is a daily reality as we write. We are only at the very beginning of a technics that is likely to be as important to the twenty-first century as the automobile was to the twentieth. This may be seen as a parody of the first Age, when maid was less physical, but may also lead to new and valuable possibilities.

INDEX

Made in United States
Troutdale, OR
01/07/2024

16783497R00087